CONTENTS

FOREWORD

These papers reflect the proceedings of a very crowded
meeting held by the Library and Information Research Group
in October 1981. The Group's intention in organising this
meeting was to indicate to the various professional groups
concerned with reading amongst young people something of
the range of investigation and practical initiative being
undertaken in the field. This we hoped would stimulate
curiousity, interest and communication among librarians in
schools and public libraries as well as teachers and practitioners and researchers in both professions. Within the
confines of a one-day meeting this meant that presentations
were inevitably brief and there was little time for detailed
discussion, but the overall objective was, I think,
achieved.

A secondary objective was to point up the many different
circumstances in which research can take place and the
conditions these impose on the nature of the work. In-house
investigation, totally internalised or externally-funded,
and full-time institutionalised investigations, are equally
valid, it was shown, in helping to construct a body of knowledge which might help developments in the field. The
opportunity was also given for researchers to learn of the
concerns of librarians and the latter to be able to assess
the value of specific findings and methods for their own needs.

The ten speakers represented in these proceedings
include a Children's Books Officer responsible for a unique
collection of research materials, three public librarians,
and a range of researchers working in different contexts.
One of these researchers worked in a British Library-
funded research centre, one in a library school, and two in
University departments engaged in externally-funded full and
part-time research. One of the public librarians reported on
an externally-funded research project which she had initiated,
and all of them had been involved in change and experiment
which relied to different extents on statistics and basic data.
They were used to interpreting these data to facilitate
effective change, but could not usually afford the luxury of
discrete, rigorous and controlled investigation which full-
time research allows. To some extent, therefore, the wheels
were already oiled for the ensuing dialogue.

The day revealed a common concern amongst librarians and researchers to find out more about the needs of young people and the influence of schools, communities and parents on the shaping of these needs. Possibly because this area has been under-researched in the past, the thirst for knowledge was strong on both sides, with little of the usual antagonism dividing researchers and practitioners being apparent. Contributors stressed the need for more dissemination of relevant work both within and outside librarianship and for an advisory facility to help those wishing to undertake research. Specific topics were mentioned as requiring more investigation, and they were ably summed up by Nick Moore at the end of the meeting. Pre-eminent amongst these were staff attitudes to change, means of determining customers' needs, patterns of use and non-use and ways of developing more effective services to schools, ethnic minorities and young people in the public library. With regard to library materials, problems of publishing and acquiring mother-tongue materials were stressed, and the need to promote an awareness of the importance of *knowing about books* amongst those able to influence young people's attitudes. Novel approaches by libraries might stimulate this realisation by, for example, integrating services for young people, including the voluntary, within a locality, or by self-publication of story-telling sessions. Such developments would be amenable to experimental research.

Requests for further meetings on specific topics only touched on here proved to the Library and Information Research Group that interest had been effectively stimulated. Either they or a specialist group within this area of library work might well respond to this call in the near future. Our experience shows that potential interest is high.

LESLEY GILDER
Centre for Library and Information Management
University of Loughborough

THE RE-DESIGN OF A COUNTY LIBRARY SERVICE TO YOUNG PEOPLE

Tony Winslade
Assistant County Librarian, Services to Schools and Young People,
Derbyshire County Library

'The lending of books, as well the smaller without pictures as the larger with pictures, is forbidden under the penalty of excommunication.'

It is perhaps as well that the learned Abbot of Croyland is not presiding over this gathering, or we may as well all go home to our own book collections - yet in that we, like the good abbot, are in a minority. The book-owning section of the population is a smaller proportion of the population even than the borrowing section and we, therefore, have a solemn duty to provide facilities and materials for up-lifting the reading habits of the public, providing for young people good quality literature and what Carlyle described as 'books to gather facts from.'

In this we have indeed been singularly successful since the beginning of public libraries, not so long after Carlyle asked 'Why is there not a Majesty's Library in every coun-try town? There is a Majesty's gaol and gallows in every one.' We congratulate ourselves that we reach a high pro-portion of the population with our services - 40% no less being registered borrowers, and our issue figures continue to increase.

At the start of this decade, prompted perhaps by the winds of economic change, this mood of self-congratulation gave way to a more questioning attitude - why weren't we reaching the other 60%? - universal education had after all raised reading standards. With this more questioning attitude came the realisation that the previous decade had brought a more dramatic though less immediately visible

4

change than even the traumatic disturbances of 1974.
Recognition of the volume of missing users brought with it
recognition of the change, in marketing terms, from a seller's
to a buyer's market - a fact which perhaps influenced the
adoption of the marketing concept in the re-assessment
of the library's services in Derbyshire.

The marketing concept defines a seller's market as one
in which the focus is on the products or service and the
criterion of success, or objective, is considered by volume
- of sales, or in our case loans - achieved by selling or
promotion. The buyer's market on the other hand is defined
as one in which the focus is on the customer and the criterion of success, or objective, is expressed in terms of
customer satisfaction achieved by marketing. Marketing,
however, is a term which is often misconstrued as merely
the promotion or 'selling' of the product or service,
whereas in reality it is a much more complex activity
carrying considerable implications for the whole structure
of the company or, in our case, service. In devising a
marketing plan one needs to examine first a wide range of
external factors to determine possible constraints, possible
areas of demand for service and, as important or perhaps
more so, to examine the strengths and weaknesses of one's
own services and the range of current services offered
before deciding upon one's objectives and strategy for
whatever change is necessary.

In Derbyshire the application of this framework showed
that the operation of various 'environmental' factors had
changed the nature of our 'market', or rather the range of
possible markets, thus raising the question of how well we
were serving the various market segments - ethnic minorities,
urban and rural disadvantaged, the gifted, the isolated,
the early and mid-teens; raising questions about the
adequacy of present services - were they of the right
type, in the correct order of priority for modern conditions?
Our organisational strengths and weaknesses - or rather
the strengths and weaknesses of our organisation -
were queried; consideration was given to the conceptions
of the service held by the 'coal-face' workers and, as
important, to the degree of match or mismatch between the
conceptions of the branch and area staffs and those of the
management. In all this analysis, the focus of attention
was the effect upon the customer.

This analysis suggested that the organisation then in operation, whilst appropriate to a seller's market, did not match the needs of a buyer's market and did not complement one of our recognised strengths, compared to other County Council Departments, which was the degree of direct contact with our customers; indeed, with its complete separation of children's and school services and the relative isolation of individual children's librarians within the area structure, that same structure could perhaps be a weakness, providing little opportunity for interaction between the expertise of the Schools Library Service and that of the children's librarians. Some instances of mis-match between the management and 'coal-face' conceptions of the service were wider than were acceptable in the development of a user-sensitive service. Certain environmental factors were crucial at this stage, including a change in the political scene and personality changes in the Education Department.

The potential market for services to young people, when analysed with the user as the focus, divided less obviously into schools and public service sectors than it had when the services were the focus.

Having made our analysis, what action was then necessary for our newly-defined overall objective of a user-sensitive service? The first was obviously to develop a managerial and administrative system related to the user, which meant a degree of dismantling of the former mutually exclusive area organisation and separate Schools Library Service, and replacing it with one through which both schools and individual young people could benefit from the expertise of both schools and public service staff.

The second was to build upon the strength of our public contact, to bring more of the staff into direct contact with the public, and to give them the objective of really knowing their public.

The third was to ensure that there was a degree of co-ordination at a high level and a facility for the more ready focusing of attention on services to young people. Indeed a change of nomenclature was one of the first results of the re-focusing upon the user rather than the service - though the concept of the 'child' still exists, it is as part of a continuum of a wide range of users who need different services at different times.

From the former area administration came two elements of service - that provided through static branches and that provided through mobiles, which together with service through schools can be grouped around a triangle of co-ordination - the Assistant County Librarian. With our expanded concept of the user overlaying this, we contain other aspects of the organisation - staffing, materials and systems - within the focal framework provided by the user.

In practical terms this has meant the development of a series of group teams based on selected larger libraries with responsibility for the development of services to young people through the public branches within a given geographical area, which in some groups is attached to a specific post, whereas in others it is a split responsibility. The Schools Library Service has been split into a supply section (still unfortunately eccentrically located) and an advisory section of field-based officers who are responsible for overseeing the standards of School Library Service, promoting effective and efficient use of library facilities in schools, and promoting co-operation and co-ordination between schools and public library-based staff.

The communications system is devised to try to ensure that all staff dealing with young peoples' services have ready access to information which they may need, whilst each division concentrates upon a particular aspect of usage. Public library-based staff seek to extend the information bank on young people as individual users of the library service, schools service-based staff concentrating upon the needs of institutions. Periodic meetings are held to promote an awareness of a whole county service and to assess the success or otherwise of the re-structuring in terms of re-focusing attention on the user, and to develop the marketing framework in terms of analysis of the market or markets and the better utilisation of our strengths.

In the marketing of any product or service there is a natural life cycle, within which are phases of introduction and development, growth, maturity and decline, and for which there is a corresponding cycle of costs - high per user at the beginning because of the effort needed to get the product or service established, decreasing as the product or service becomes established and increasing again as efforts are needed to maintain the service or product when alternative sources begin to develop. In the re-structured services to young people in Derbyshire we are faced with high costs of development, related particularly to book knowledge, on the part of the new, young and relatively inexperienced staff who hold responsibility for services to young people in these groups, changing attitudes of those who still see young people as children, and overcoming a quarter of a century of traditional separation of services to young people in and out of school. In recent years certain initiatives have been taken to break through this separation and to develop services related to user needs, such as the Book Bus scheme for urban areas of deprivation and social priority (begun with an urban aid grant in 1977), and its corollary, the Holiday Book Special, a public library mobile service using School Library Service mobiles during the Summer holiday, and deliberately focused on countering rural deprivation.

When the criterion of success is volume of sales or use, analysis and presentation of success or otherwise is simple - records of issues and number and variety of registered borrowers are easily understood by librarians and lay persons. Evaluation of the success of the redesigned services to young people in Derbyshire will be more difficult and offers ample scope for research, most notably into the assessment of customer satisfaction, into possible means of changing staff attitudes, and into determination of what the customer really wants from the service. Which brings us back to the point at which I started - a service whose focus is the product rather than the user - and raises the philosophical question of whether we should or should not provide what such research would reveal as being required.

PROMOTIONAL ACTIVITIES AND MATERIALS IN WORK WITH CHILDREN

Margaret Fearn

Lecturer,
Department of Library and Information Studies,
University of Loughborough

It would seem reasonable to agree with Pauline Wilson in a recent paper on American children's libraries that 'for any profession there are two sources of power - organisation and knowledge'. Her view that 'children's librarians have too limited a view of the intellectual content of their field' (1) has now, however, thankfully been overtaken by the increasing interest shown both here and in the United States in researching library work with children.

Nevertheless in the past there has been very little published research in this field in the U.K., so that, paradoxically, deciding on the priorities for an enquiry is exceedingly difficult when focusing on areas relevant to children's librarians. We understand so little about the way in which children use their public library, other than in the most general terms, that each of several lines of enquiry seems of the utmost and urgent importance in enlarging our understanding.

1. *What is the pattern of library use and non-use by children at different ages and stages of development, from the pre-school child to the adolescent?*

   When do they visit the library, with whom, and for what purpose? The Whitehead survey (2) only touched upon this area when looking at children's choice of reading, while recent studies of public library use (3) have tended to skirt the problem.

2.   *What happens to children in the public library?*

What do they do in the library? What kind of
relationships develop between children and staff,
both professional and non-professional? What do
children borrow and what do they read as a result
of visiting the library? The two are not necessarily identical.

3.   *What part does the public library play in the
school/parent/public library trinity of
influences affecting children's reading habits?*

The Bullock report (4) made great play with the
importance of all three in improving children's
reading in the early years, but we have little
hard evidence of the impact of public libraries.
There is, however, ample evidence of both the
school and parental role in shaping children's
reading (5).

4.   *What perception do children have of the public
library?*

While it is now customary in studies of the
reading habits of older children (10+) (6) to
question them fairly thoroughly on their choice
of books, the same exercise has not been carried
out with regard to their choice of venue for
borrowing books, and their views on public libraries in particular, although Pauline Heather's
recent study (7) paints a depressing picture of
attitudes held by some teenagers. Recent work on
the psychology of childhood would also suggest
that as young children from about the ages of 5
or 6 are capable of genuinely philosophical
thought, we ought to pay much more heed to the
considered views of these younger children (8).

These are some very large questions, which can be
answered only by a number of research projects over a
considerable period of time. It was therefore a very real
problem to decide which area to look at in some depth when
embarking on research in children's librarianship. What
did seem important, however, in a field which had seen
very little academic enquiry, was some scrutiny of a

methodology appropriate not simply for one topic but having some general application. In order to begin looking at some of the methodological problems in researching children's librarianship, therefore, and at the same time to examine one specific area, it was decided that an analysis of promotional activities and materials in an inner-city branch library (9) would be particularly appropriate. The promotion of the public library service and of reading encroaches upon all four of the broad lines of enquiry isolated above, so that methods which were used in this project might be useful as a means of developing a methodology for research in the field as a whole. The aims of this project were therefore twofold, firstly to look at promotion and secondly at the problems of evaluation.

Promotion of the library service to children is not new, and is of course in a sense always the concern of librarians. However, activities which were once considered merely as 'extension activities' (10) have now become a means of promoting the concept of the library as a social venue for children, and at the same time of encouraging them to take part in a range of events. These are no longer at the periphery of the library service but play an integral part and may be craft or drama-related, or more conventionally book-related activities such as story-telling (the range of activities now available in librar-ies is extremely wide and it is difficult to categorise them other than in these general terms). Similarly, publicity materials for children's activities are not new, but their impact and an assessment of their usefulness in advertising the library to children had not previously been undertaken. Having decided on an area that had not previously been examined in any depth and that had important implications for other areas of children's librarianship, the first question regarding the approach to be adopted could be posed.

How should the research be orientated?

Would a quantitative assessment be the most useful basis for the study, examining the numbers of children involved, quantities of books issued and read? Or should the emphasis be rather on the qualitative aspects of the impact, examining who the children were and why they attended activities, what they had gained from the experience and read as a result?

The numbers of children responding to publicity and
attending the library either as new or existing members
and the number of books issued would be an obvious measure
of the success or failure of promotion. As the personal
fulfilment of children in both attending activities and in
any reading they might do was an equally important measure
of success, however, these outcomes could not be ignored.
It seemed important therefore to attempt a balance between
the two approaches, as both were relevant to the enquiry.

The second question regarding approaches to the enquiry
followed naturally from the response to the first:

*What data should be gathered in order to achieve this
balance between quantitative and qualitative assessment?*

The quantitative data seemed at first sight to be
straightforward - membership and issues, and the numbers
of children receiving publicity materials and attending
activities - although as we later discovered, some of
these measurements were not particularly helpful as
indicators of library use. The qualitative assessment was,
however, an especially interesting problem since there
were no guidelines within previous library research relevant to our examination of the kinds of activity being
provided for children within libraries. It was important
firstly that we described as accurately and objectively
as possible what was taking place, in order to compare
activities, and secondly that we attempted to evaluate
the effectiveness of the activity. While educational
research, particularly the work of Flanders and the
methods used in the Oracle project (11), provided interesting
models for the objective observation of activities, it was
necessary to tailor these to the special needs of library
work with children, and to relate them to the objectives
set by librarians for the evaluation of activities.

In addition to observation, the views of children in
the library and at school were canvassed in order to
discover their attitudes towards the public library,
promotional activities and reading, and the impact of the
publicity materials. Since we were looking at children
aged between 7 and 11 years this involved structured interviewing with many young children, all of whom responded
extremely well and were forthright in their comments.

It became evident as the project continued that achieving a balance between the two approaches, quantitative and qualitative, was a major feature of this kind of research. It was impossible to measure objectively without posing subjective questions, or more often having the questions posed for the researcher by librarians and children. Similarly, the subjective impressions we gained could be confirmed, rejected, or more usually modified as a result of hard data.

Essentially, the methods used in this project were very closely tied to the stated objectives of the librarians working with children, and these objectives are of course likely to change in line with children's needs. Any overall research methodology for use in library work with children should therefore be flexible enough to meet the needs of this constant development. The kind of quantitative measures required today might no longer be simply membership and issue data but relate much more to attendance at the library and requests for information.

As we were using traditional measures it was possible only to glimpse the use made of the library by children who were non-members, but it seems probable that this forms quite a high percentage of the overall attendance at the library - certainly in this particular community. We need to develop many more techniques for the quantitative and qualitative assessment of these aspects of library use - particularly with regard to encounters between children and library staff during activity sessions, user education lessons, library visits and routine day-to-day enquiry work.

There is real opportunity here for collaboration between children's librarians and researchers. By defining the aims and objectives of the library service in quite specific ways, librarians can help to develop a methodology which is in keeping with practice. There is a danger that research can proceed within certain normative parameters regarding library work with children, for example that liaison between primary schools and public libraries is always fruitful. When looking rather more closely at the operation of liaison in the regular school visits to the library, after discussing these in some detail with children's librarians, quite a different perspective could be gained. How productive is a library visit when children are frog-marched to the library by a teacher, who orders them to select two books each, waits silently while they chaotically do so, and then leads them back to school? It does of course

provide children with the opportunity to acquire two books
to read, but haphazardly selected and with little time for
the librarian to guide a hesitant reader. The short-term
gain of providing some reading material for these children
may be outweighed by the long-term loss of a more positive
image of the public library as a place where reading can
be an enjoyable experience and a child may lose himself
in a book.

By discussing such relationships in some depth, the
researcher and librarian are led to a clearer mutual
understanding of the distance between current practice
and the eventual achievement of objectives. It is then
possible to provide properly relevant methods for research
and useful findings and recommendations. If we are finally
to confound Pauline Wilson's argument that children's
librarians have only a limited view of the intellectual
content of their field, we must develop co-operation
between research and practice in order to achieve better
organisation and wider knowledge, the sources of power
for children's library services.

REFERENCES

1. WILSON, P. Children's services and power: knowledge
    to shape the future. *Top of the News*, 37(2), 1981,
    pp. 115-125.

2. WHITEHEAD, F. *Children and their books (Schools Council
    Research Studies)*. London: Macmillan Education, 1977.

3. LUCKHAM, B. *The library in society*. London: The
    Library Association, 1971.

    TOTTERDELL, B; *The effective library*. London: The
    Library Association, 1976.

4. GREAT BRITAIN, Department of Education and Science.
    A language for life. London: H.M.S.O., 1975, pp.
    98-99.

5. SOUTHGATE, V. *Extending beginning reading*. London:
    Heinemann, 1981.

    HEWISON, J. Parental involvement and reading attain-
    ment. *British Journal of Educational Psychology*, 50,
    1980, pp. 209-15.

14

6. WHITEHEAD, op. cit., pp 29–33, 162–175.

7. HEATHER, P. *Young people's reading; a study of the leisure reading of 13–15 year olds.* Sheffield: Centre for Research on User Studies, 1981, pp. 19–29.

8. MATTHEWS, B. *Philosophy and the young child.* Cambridge, Mass.: Harvard University Press, 1980.

9. FEARN, M. *Promotional activities and materials in work with children in an inner-city branch library* to be published shortly by the Centre for Library and Information Management, Department of Library and Information Studies, Loughborough University, Loughborough, Leics.

10. HARROD, L.M. *Library work with children.* London: Deutsch, 1969, p. 44.

11. FLANDERS, N.A. *Analyzing teaching behaviour.* Reading, Mass.: Addison-Wesley, 1970.

    GALTON, M. *Inside the primary classroom.* London: Routledge and Kegan Paul, 1980.

THE BOOKMASTER PROJECT

Lorna Roberts
Head of Children's and Youth Services,
Westminster Public Libraries

It was a feeling of guilt that really prompted us to
go for a research grant. Over the years the activities
programme and the growth of reading schemes had created a
situation in our libraries in which children of all age
groups were enthusiastically reading books and talking
about their reactions. We learnt so much each summer that
we regarded participation in it as an essential part of
staff training. The schemes had been monitored from the
beginning, so we had built up a wealth of background
material. The final impetus was the development of the
Bookmaster scheme.

In the Bookworm scheme the children discuss the books
they have read with staff. We all learn from this exchange
of opinions, and staff are encouraged to keep notes and
add them to the final report on the scheme. There are two
problems with this; firstly that not everything is recorded,
and less-experienced staff may not realise the importance of something that might be said. Also, with verbal
communication it was difficult to ensure when talking to
a reader that you were not influencing their reaction.
When we found books which caused problems, we had difficulty in framing questions which did not indicate a
preferred answer. Bookmaster was deliberately devised for
good readers of 11 - 18, who had outgrown Bookworm, and
we incorporated the idea of reviews written by children
in order to obtain material which could be analysed and
compared. Having got the reviews, and realising they
offered important clues to teenage reading, we simply had
to do something with them so that all Westminster staff
could benefit.

The Report for 1979 was written to make the material available to a wider audience, and as documentary evidence to back up a proposal for a research grant. We initially started discussion with the British Library in January 1980. It was suggested that our proposal fell within the scope of the British National Bibliography (B.N.B.) Research and Development Fund, and it was passed to them. We have had a very useful relationship with the staff of the B.N.B. ever since, and are grateful to them for the help and interest they have shown in our project.

Although there was the opportunity to investigate any or all of the age groups from 2 to 18, we decided to limit it to the 11 - 18 age group. This was partly because of the fact that this coincided with Bookmaster, but mostly because this is the age group that most commonly drops out of libraries and reading, and the information already collected indicated some of the possible reasons.

There was no possibility of taking on the research internally. Over the summer the children's libraries team are totally involved in the organisation of the Bookworm and Activities programme, and all other work is dropped. Other sections of the library service give what help they can. I wrote the 1979 and the 1980 Bookmaster Reports from material collected by staff, and most of this work was done in my 'spare' time. There was simply no way of finding staff time to set up and carry out a research project. Additionally, as I had found from writing the reports, our close involvement made it impossible to take an outsider's view. I was too aware of the dedicated work of the staff, and knew too many of the children, to be coldly critical of their work. Someone outside the staff could exploit the situation created by the Bookmaster scheme to explore teenage reading, and evaluate the advantages, if any, of such schemes in encouraging reading.

The proposal therefore, was to investigate the reading needs and preferences of teenagers, using Westminster's eight main children's libraries during the summer when the schemes are in operation.

Following discussion with the staff of B.N.B., our first tentative proposal was revised and enlarged, but delays meant that the original aim of carrying out the research in the summer of 1980 was not possible. Instead,

it was suggested that we should mount a seminar jointly
with the National Book League, to disseminate the findings
of the Bookmaster Report. This occurred in March 1981, and
referred to the 1980 Bookmaster Report. This did help, as
it indicated something of the range of interests in teenage reading, and the kind of questions being raised. We
were informed verbally of the success of our application
in March 1981, and later obtained written confirmation.
Unfortunately, at this stage there was further delay, since
Local Government restrictions meant that we had to obtain
committee approval for an apparent increase in both staffing
and expenditure.

As someone new to research, I found this the most
difficult period. With so much work to be accomplished
before the summer, plans had to be made. Yet until written
confirmation was received from the B.N.B. and approval
obtained from Westminster City Council, certain approaches
were blocked. In all discussions with possible research
workers, I was under strict instructions to avoid making
any statements which could be misunderstood as verbal
agreement.

At these first discussions I also became aware of the
very different approach of the practical librarian and
the research worker. We had already undertaken a number of
small in-house research projects into aspects of our work.
With limited staff our approach was strictly practical. We
needed to find out information on a section of our work.
If we could devise a method which took up a specified
amount of staff time, then the project could go ahead. Our
proposal had been framed in this way. Research workers, I
discovered, approached the work from the opposite direction.
They estimated the work involved, and the time needed to
explore the various possibilities as fully as possible.
Our proposal was time-limited from the start, but I quickly
realised that the research workers' approach showed that
far more time would be needed than anticipated.

We were very fortunate that Jean Bird agreed to undertake our research. Since she lived in Westminster, she had
the added advantage of understanding the special problems
presented by the international community, and the vast
differences in economic backgrounds. A small steering group
was set up consisting of Roy Brown, Deputy City Librarian
and a member of the Public Libraries Research Group; Gordon
Eynon, Assistant City Librarian (Administration); Jean Bird,

and myself. Thus were we able to sort out aims and objectives, and the feasibility of the actual work to be undertaken.

It was understood from the beginning that all members of the Children's Libraries team would be kept fully informed about the research, and would undertake some of the work if needed. Data were collected by means of questionnaires and in-depth recorded interviews. Staff helped in piloting, and in the completion of the questionnaires. They also helped to select teenagers for the interviews, and in the provision of background information on the community using their library. The population of the survey was the 11 - 18 age group who used the children's libraries during the 8 weeks of the Bookmaster Scheme. This included teenagers who were enrolled in Bookmaster, Bookwizard and Bookworm, and those using the libraries but not enrolled in any scheme. Bookmaster has always been publicised as a scheme whereby teenagers can help their library choose books they would enjoy seeing on the shelves. We publicised the research project as yet another means of them helping us to give them a better library, and most treated the questionnaires and interviews very seriously. The research project was limited to the Children's Libraries because of the impossibility of finding sufficient staff time to extend it to cover all service points. Although irked at times by this limitation, it was felt that the information gained would help in formulating a more extensive future research project involving all of the libraries. May I add that total coverage in Westminster would have to include the monitoring of a range of specialist separate libraries such as the reference libraries, the Central Music Library and the Archive sections.

The research project has produced a wealth of data. The questionnaires have been processed and analysed by computer, and with 489 completed and usable questionnaires, we were very close to the 500 top limit. The in-depth interviews were extensive and provided more detailed material to be analysed. We have information on the preferences of this age group, the things they look for in books and in libraries, the schools they attend and the distances they travel to the library they use. There is information on their background, and the languages used at home. Jean Bird has just completed her report, which will be presented to the B.N.B. Committee in December 1981. We hope it will be published in 1982. After some discussion, we decided to produce a 1981

Bookmaster Report to fill in some details of the schemes
operating in Westminster and to complement the research
report. It will be interesting to see if the more subjective
deductions drawn from the Bookmaster reviews are confirmed
by the more analytical research report.

The information collected during the research project
should have implications for publishers, teachers,
librarians and parents. Westminster has a very varied
socio-economic community, including some of the richest
families in the country and some of the most deprived. We
have children from multi-millionaire families, and children
from hostels for the homeless. We are an international
community, with children from every country in the world
visiting Westminster at some stage. Some are residents
for many years, others live here only briefly. We have large
communities from Hong-Kong, Spain, Japan, Morocco and the
Philippines, to name but a few. Many of our West Indian and
Asian children are second and third generation Londoners,
while new residents may come from Ireland, Scotland or
Wales.

This rich and varied background means that within our
community are examples of many problems faced by teenagers
approaching libraries and books. Some have English as a
second language. In some homes there are few books, and
parents lack interest in their children's reading and
education. Many have lived in a number of countries, and
have attended a variety of schools. They are inner city
children, aware of both the dangers and the delights of
city living, and are often very mature and adult in their
approach.

This has proved to be a very interesting, if at times
nerve-racking year. Like most people, I would like to be
starting again, but with the information and experience
already gained. I consider the research project to have
been successful, and it has provided the information we
hoped for. All the staff of the children's libraries have
gained immeasurably by their association with the research.
It has been hard work, but we have all learned from Jean
Bird, as she has guided us through the project. Jean made
us define our objectives in the realistic situation, she
introduced us to the piloting of questionnaires, and to
the traumas of completing the final questionnaires in the
correct market research manner.

As the person most involved with the administration and organisation side, I think the most important thing I learned was the swift passage of time. Whether it is in planning the timetable of research, or the actual operation, I now cynically think that the best way is to make a first estimate, then double or treble the time thought necessary. The problem is that, as experienced librarians,·we know the time needed for most routine work, and get used to cutting corners if time gets short. There are no short cuts in research, and the first and the last questionnaire will take the same amount of time. One is therefore in a situation where all the work is new to your staff, and takes longer than anticipated, and additionally, most of the work will not become easier or quicker to do.

I work in a team situation, and feel it is my first priority to keep all members of my staff informed. This becomes a major time-consumer in research, especially if staff are playing an active role, and need training. I found it helpful to have a steering committee of senior staff who could answer for their departments. We avalanched the Administration Department with demands for duplicated material, and needed Gordon Eynon to agree to what was feasible, and to plan a timetable with his staff. Too few library staff ever get the opportunity to see research in action; it is a marvellous training exercise, and well worth the time lost to routine work.

My final comment is on the problems of a library devising, initiating, and carrying out research. I have had experience of small scale in-house research and found it useful and productive. Larger scale research with the guidance of a research worker is beneficial to all. The problem is getting started, and finding out about available research workers. We were lucky, but it seems a very hit-and-miss situation. The problems with making earlier links are simply that you dare not make definite arrangements until the grant is finalised and cleared. No research worker can afford to wait in limbo indefinitely. I think it would be helpful if somebody, such as the Public Libraries Research Group or the Library and Information Research Group, could set up a standing committee who could offer help to libraries with ideas, and maintain a register of researchers and their interests. There have been many times in the last two years when the difficulties have mounted, and when it hardly seemed worth while continuing. To have had in the background a body able to give disinterested advice and help would have been most encouraging.

REFERENCE

Details of methods used, results and conclusions of this project are given in the report:

BIRD, Jean. *Bookmaster and the teenage reader*. To be published by or on behalf of the British National Bibliography Research Fund, 1982.

A LONGITUDINAL STUDY OF THE READING
HABITS OF 13-15 YEAR OLDS

Pauline Heather
Research Assistant,
Centre for Research on User Studies,
University of Sheffield

First, the context in which this research was conducted.
The Centre for Research on User Studies (usually
shortened to CRUS) at Sheffield University is one of
several research units funded by the British Library, and
research on young people's reading is part of the Centre's
school programme. Our other research programmes are concerned with academic libraries and public libraries. The
schools programme also includes the following projects:-

1.   A survey of the methods by which teachers select
      books. 136 teachers from both primary and secondary
      schools were interviewed, covering the complete
      range of subjects. The study (1) found that
      teachers were often bewildered by the array of
      information sources at their disposal, and their
      choice of sources was often haphazard or arbitrary.
      The survey makes suggestions for improvements
      in the quality of information sources, and
      also recommends that guidance on book selection
      be included in initial teacher training courses
      and in-service courses. It was found that the
      information sources which were most commonly
      used, i.e. publishers' catalogues and representatives,
      were not held to be the most useful: teachers who
      attended exhibitions and a display bookroom found
      these sources of greater value. The survey was
      conducted in Sheffield and Rotherham, and some of
      the findings might therefore not be applicable to
      other areas which have different systems - for example,
      the Inner London Education Authority, where publishers'

representatives are not permitted to visit schools.

2.   A forthcoming project will be concerned with
      primary school children and libraries; the project
      is in the early stages of development. A meeting
      of people with involvement in primary school
      libraries, including one of the few professional
      primary school librarians, has been held at CRUS
      as an initial step in its development, and the
      next stage of the project is likely to be visits
      to several primary schools to discuss the practical
      issues of promoting library use among primary
      school children. Structured observation in class-
      rooms is being considered as a possible research
      method for the project. This may reveal which
      methods of teaching result in pupils finding out
      information for themselves, and at what ages
      pupils are ready to learn different library skills.

3.   A third schools project involves all members of
      staff at the centre; designated 'Library Access
      and Sixth Form Studies' it has been undertaken
      jointly with the Centre for Applied Research in
      Education at the University of East Anglia. The
      project's aim was to discover teachers' and
      students' perceptions of library provision for
      their teaching and studying. Each researcher on
      the project was allocated an educational institu-
      tion with a sixth form, i.e. school, sixth form
      college or college of further education, and
      spent two weeks interviewing and observing mem-
      bers of staff and students. The interviews were
      unstructured and tape recorded; transcripts from
      the interviews were indexed by the appropriate
      researcher. Preparation of the project report
      will begin shortly.

The approach chosen for the project under review was
the monitoring of the reading habits of a sample of young
people over a period of time. If the subjects were to be
interviewed several times at frequent intervals, their
numbers had to be limited; the disadvantages of the small
size of the sample were considered to be balanced by the
detail of the information that would be gathered. The
sample consisted of a total of 60 pupils who came from 10
local schools; these pupils were in their third year of
secondary education at the start of the study, and were

interviewed once a term for five terms, i.e. nearly two
years. The pupils were provided with notebooks in which to
write down the titles of any books which they had read
voluntarily. This proved successful; it was mainly the pupils
who had not read many books who lost their 'reading diaries'.
The pupils were asked questions about the books they had read
at each interview. They were also asked about the magazines
which they read and how they spent their free time.

Some findings from the study, illustrated here with
references from some of the case studies in the report, are
indicative. It was found that the number of books read de-
clined as the pupils grew older. Contrary to expectations,
the number of pupils overall who read books did not
decrease during the study; some pupils stopped reading, but
equally others started. By looking in more detail at one
of the pupils, 'Louise', who had started reading, it may
be possible to shed light on how other teenagers can be
encouraged to start reading:

> Louise goes to a disco at a youth club once a week and
> also to Ambulance Cadets. She said she never read books
> because she could not find the time, although she read
> *My Guy*, and *Blue Jeans* magazines regularly. Half-way
> through the study, Louise's sister suggested that she
> read a *A Kind of Loving* by Stan Barstow. Louise enjoyed
> this book because the characters were 'like people
> we know, about everyday living'. She then borrowed two
> books from the public library, *Run for your life* by
> Line which she enjoyed because 'there weren't long
> paragraphs and there was more talking', and the other
> *Kes*, enjoyed because it was realistic. Louise was
> still reading at the time of the last interview, a
> book recommended and lent to her by her mother.

Some of the pupils who were avid readers at the start
of the study read only one type of book; most of them were
reading less by the end of the study because they were
having difficulties finding more books of the same type to
read. Matthew was one of these pupils:

> Matthew's hobbies were building models and collecting
> coins. During the study he took up war gaming and
> bought the magazine *Wings* for part of the time. His
> reading reflected his interest in war. Matthew started
> by reading science fiction and both fiction and non-
> fiction books on war. He read avidly, having always

read more than 10 books between interviews, until the
last interview. He no longer read any science fiction
books after the second interview: at the last interview Matthew said he was reading less because he was
becoming more 'choosey' about what he read. Most of
the books he had read were factual descriptions of
weapons and battles.

We thought that lack of time would be one of the main
reasons why some pupils did not read books, and were
therefore surprised to find in the course of the study
that pupils tend to read less rather than more in the
summer holidays, when they are free from homework. Also,
the keen readers seemed to find time for many other
activities as well. Cherry is an example of a keen, con-
sistent reader, with many other leisure activities:

Cherry goes to a youth club once a week and spends
time gardening, horse-riding and doing gym exercises.
During the study she started playing badminton. Cherry
read between 8 and 12 books in each period of the study,
which included several Catherine Cookson books and two
Agatha Christie books recommended by her parents. She
also liked reading animal books, and read several James
Herriott books, three by Joy Adamson, and a book of
horse stories. Her reading also varied over Richard
Gordon books and horror books by James Herbert;
several books read had been recommended by friends.
Included in her reading were many novels written for
teenagers.

To investigate the most popular books, a list was made
of all those read by more than one pupil during the study.
This consisted of a list of 50 titles, the most popular
being James Herriott's *Vet in Harness*, which had been
read by 8 pupils. James Herriott and Iam Fleming both
appear eight times in the list, and others mentioned more
than once are Isaac Asimov, James Herbert and Tolkein.
More than half the books on the list have some link with
television or films.

Pupils were asked where they had obtained each book
they had read. The replies indicated that school libraries
were not a popular source of books. The three main
sources of books were purchase, borrowing from the public
library, and borrowing from friends or family. 27% of the

26

books had been bought, 25% had been borrowed from the public
library and 24% had been borrowed from friends or family.
Only 11% of the books had been borrowed from a school
library and 10% had been received as presents. A third of
all the books bought came from W.H. Smith. Besides book-
shops, other places where books were bought included
jumble sales, book clubs, newsagents, Boots, Woolworth,
a toyshop, supermarkets, a café, and a motorway service
station. Some pupils said that they had read books because
they had been readily available; for example one pupil
said 'I felt like a change and it was convenient', and
another pupil remarked that 'it was lying around at home'.
The importance of books being readily accessible to young
people in the places where they usually go, is perhaps
underlined by these responses. In some schools the pupils
had been attracted into the school library because the
library stocked a teenage magazine. At the start of the
study 78% of the pupils said they read magazines regularly.
Although there was a slight decline in the number of
magazines read throughout the study, this was not as
marked as the decline in book reading.

The final report of the research (2) describes these
and other findings in more detail, and includes sixteen
case studies.

REFERENCES

1. VINCENT, Kate. *A survey of the methods by which
   teachers select books*. Sheffield: Centre for
   Research on User Studies, 1980 (CRUS Occasional
   Paper No. 3). (BLRDD Report No. 5549).

2. HEATHER, Pauline. *Young peoples reading: a study of
   the leisure reading of 13-15 year olds*. Sheffield:
   Centre for Research on User Studies, 1981. (CRUS
   Occasional Paper No. 6). (BLR&DD Report No. 5750).

SCHOOL ORGANISATION : ITS EFFECTS ON READING HABITS IN THE 'BRADFORD BOOK FLOOD EXPERIMENT'

Jennie Ingham
Research Fellow,
Department of Education and Performance Arts,
Middlesex Polytechnic

INTRODUCTION

The aim of 'The Bradford Book Flood Experiment' (1976-80) was to examine longitudinally the effects, upon children's reading skills, attitudes, habits and interests, of 'flooding' or saturating their classrooms with books in addition to their usual school text-books and reading books. Advisers selected two matched pairs of middle schools (9-13 years), one pair in the inner city, where the intake included a substantial proportion of children of Asian origin, the other in the outer city in an 'estate desert' area. One school in each pair was randomly designated the experimental school, thus receiving publishers' donations of approximately 5,000 books per school, in the proportions one third non-fiction to two thirds fiction; the other two schools became the controls.

The impact of the influx of books was monitored using a multi-methodological approach, ranging from the purely quantitative to the ethnographic:

a)   a battery of tests was administered, including the Edinburgh Reading Test Stage 3, the Schonell Word Recognition Test (Shearer's Revised Word Order-1975), and a non-verbal I.Q. test, Cattell's Culture Fair Test of 'g', in a pre-test/post-test design.

b)   a longitudinal record was kept of all the children's reading for the duration of the experiment (n=360), by means of a questionnaire, 'The Ingham-Clift Reading Record Form', which the children completed each time they read a book (Ingham 1981) (see Appendix 1 of present paper).

c)   case studies were conducted with approximately 10% of the sample, this sub-sample consisting of representatives of avid and infrequent readers, chosen on the basis of Reading Record Form returns and teachers' and self reports. The author interviewed each child in school and, subsequently, each set of parents in their own home, both sets of interviews being tape-recorded and afterwards transcribed.

d)   Since only four schools were involved, it was possible to record in detail factors other than the influx of books which might operate as variables affecting the outcome of the experiment. Therefore, data were collected via participant observation and in-depth interviews with school staff; it was felt that these would be of particular interest to other teachers and head-teachers reading the report.

In particular, it seemed important to record:

(i)   the way in which staff were allocated to the teaching of English, and to ascertain whether that allocation bore any relationship to the extent of the teachers' knowledge of children's books or degree of enthusiasm for them, or to their skill in display, promotion and use of books.

(ii) the timetabling of English lessons.

(iii) the allocation of classrooms to English teaching.

(iv) the organisation and use of the school library and class libraries if any, and allocation of staff to the school library.

(v)   the distribution of capitation allowance.

(vi) most importantly, the attitude of the head-teacher towards reading, because this is the single factor which, given the autonomy of the head-teacher in this country, frequently determines all the other conditions listed, especially in the middle school which is a relatively small institution.

The results of the testing programme and the Reading Record Form analysis were more favourable in the inner city than in the outer city experimental school. The test results were subjected to analysis of co-variance and

regression analysis. Five out of the six positive, statisti-
cally significant results were concerned with the effect
of the Book Flood on the reading skills of the children in
the inner city experimental school. It is worth describing
the results of the Reading Record Form analysis in greater
detail:

a)   only in the outer city experimental school did
     the number of Reading Record Forms completed
     actually *decrease* during the course of the
     experiment.

b)   in addition, the variety of books read, i.e. the
     number of individual authors and separate titles
     recorded, for the outer city experimental school
     also decreased, despite the variety of books
     introduced (see Tables 1 and 2).

Table 1. Number of Reading Record Forms completed: outer
         city schools (matched schools paired)

No. of Reading Record Forms	10+ Exp. Frequency	Con.	11+ Exp. Frequency	Con.	12+ Exp. Frequency	Con.
60–64						
55–59						
50–54						
45–49						
40–44				1		
35–39				1		
30–34	2			3	1	
25–29	2			2	O	
20–24	12		3	1	O	2
15–19	18	1	15	4	1	11
10–14	27	6	22	10	13	24
5–9	12	39	23	26	31	38
0–4	4	37	11	32	24	4
Totals	1095	447	773	666	456	782
n=	(77)	(83)	(74)	(80)	(70)	(70)

Table 2. Number of Reading Record Forms completed: inner
city schools (matched schools paired)

No. of Reading Record Forms	10+ Exp. Frequency	10+ Con. Frequency	11+ Exp. Frequency	11+ Con. Frequency	12+ Exp. Frequency	12+ Con. Frequency
60–64					1	
55–59					O	
50–54					1	
45–49					O	
40–44					1	
35–39					O	
30–34		1			4	2
25–29	2	O	2		8	7
20–24	4	1	6		9	7
15–19	6	5	5	1	12	26
10–14	19	14	13	17	16	28
5–9	37	30	25	43	19	12
0–4	26	45	38	25	15	1
Totals	776	590	688	582	1240	1250
n=	(94)	(94)	(89)	(86)	(86)	(83)

c)   whilst there was an increase in sheer numbers of
Reading Record Forms completed for both the inner
city experimental *and control* schools, in the
control school there was an increase of only 16
titles, and *a decrease* of authors recorded (i.e.
the children in the inner city control school
were doing a great deal of reading at the end
of the experiment, reading as much in terms of
numbers of books as the children in the matched
experimental school, but were reading no greater
variety of books than at the beginning); whereas

the children in the inner city experimental school
more than doubled the number of titles recorded,
and almost doubled the number of individual authors
recorded (see Tables 3 and 4).

Table 3. Number of individual titles recorded in each
school in each year

Outer city schools

	10+		11+		12+	
	Exp.	Con.	Exp.	Con.	Exp.	Con.
No. of titles	554	290	471	322	249	307
No. of returns	1095	447	773	666	456	782
n=	(77)	(83)	(74)	(80)	(70)	(79)

Inner city schools

	10+		11+		12+	
	Exp.	Con.	Exp.	Con.	Exp.	Con.
No. of titles	415	404	479	299	886	412
No. of returns	776	590	688	582	1240	1250
n=	(94)	(94)	(89)	(86)	(86)	(83)

Table 4. Number of individual authors recorded in each
          school in each year

Outer city schools

	10+		11+		12+	
	Exp.	Con.	Exp.	Con.	Exp.	Con.
No. of author	343	196	314	199	244	272
No. of returns	1095	447	773	666	456	782
n=	(77)	(83)	(74)	(80)	(70)	(79)

Inner city schools

	10+		11+		12+	
	Exp.	Con.	Exp.	Con.	Exp.	Con.
No. of authors	274	273	311	157	500	228
No. of returns	776	590	688	582	1240	1250
n=	(94)	(94)	(89)	(86)	(86)	(83)

d)   in the inner city experimental school alone did
     the children record more books enjoyed as the
     experiment progressed. Indeed, in every case, i.e.
     for boys and girls together and separately, the
     percentage of books enjoyed increased each year
     throughout the experiment. (see Table 5).

Table 5. Number of times books rated as 1 or 2 in Question 5
(Ingham-Clift Reading Record Form), set against total
Reading Record Form returns, by school, year, and sex.

Outer city experimental school

	Boys & Girls	Boys	Girls	Boys & Girls	Boys	Girls	Boys & Girls	Boys	Girls
	10+	10+	10+	11+	11+	11+	12+	12+	12+
Total returns	1095	596	499	773	383	390	456	230	226
No. rated as 1 or 2	598	321	277	388	198	190	185	104	81
% rated as 1 or 2	54.6	53.9	55.5	50.2	51.7	48.7	40.6	45.2	35.8
n=	(77)	(39)	(38)	(74)	(39)	(35)	(70)	(38)	(32)

Outer city control school

	Boys & Girls	Boys	Girls	Boys & Girls	Boys	Girls	Boys & Girls	Boys	Girls
	10+	10+	10+	11+	11+	11+	12+	12+	12+
Total returns	447	241	206	666	328	338	782	421	361
No. rated as 1 or 2	250	135	115	306	147	159	329	165	164
% rated as 1 or 2	55.9	50.0	55.8	45.9	44.8	47.0	42.1	39.2	45.4
n=	(83)	(46)	(37)	(80)	(46)	(34)	(79)	(46)	(33)

Inner city experimental school

	Boys & Girls	Boys	Girls	Boys & Girls	Boys	Girls	Boys & Girls	Boys	Girls
	10+	10+	10+	11+	11+	11+	12+	12+	12+
Total returns	776	378	398	688	372	316	1240	704	536
No. rated as 1 or 2	478	235	243	450	239	211	827	464	363
% rated as 1 or 2	61.6	62.2	61.1	65.4	64.3	66.8	66.7	65.9	67.1
n=	(94)	(51)	(43)	(89)	(49)	(46)	(86)	(48)	(38)

Inner city control school

	Boys & Girls	Boys	Girls	Boys & Girls	Boys	Girls	Boys & Girls	Boys	Girls
	10+	10+	10+	11+	11+	11+	12+	12+	12+
Total returns	590	170	420	582	224	358	1250	492	758
Rated as 1 or 2	306	86	220	375	137	238	597	257	340
% rated as 1 or 2	51.9	50.6	52.4	64.4	61.2	66.5	47.8	52.2	44.9
n=	(94)	(39)	(55)	(86)	(37)	(49)	(83)	(35)	(48)

We must ask ourselves why the influx of books was so
efficacious in the inner city experimental school and not
in its outer city counterpart; and how the inner city
control school did so much to encourage reading with a far
poorer stock of books, and less choice. The results would
seem to suggest that the availability of a large number
and wide variety of books is a necessary but not sufficient
condition if children are to read widely. It seems
likely that the other necessary condition, apart from the
availability of a large number and wide variety of books,
and a condition which pertained in *both* inner city schools,
is an environment conducive to the full use of those books
by the children. Only in the inner city experimental
school did these two necessary conditions come together.
Variety is important because it gives more opportunity for
a child to find something to his taste, and facilitates
the development of discriminatory powers. It is when we
look at the differences in organisation of the two experimental schools that we find clues as to why the Book Flood
affected one so much more favourably than the other.

ALLOCATION OF STAFF TO ENGLISH TEACHING

In the outer city experimental school, English was
taught throughout the school by class teachers, a policy
determined by the Headmaster (which may be, in part, a
reflection of the junior school origin of this particular
middle school). The children were extracted for remedial
work, however, and in addition the Head of English had
been in the habit of withdrawing a group, usually of the
most able children, for perhaps half a term at a time,
for part of their English work, so that most of the children in the school did receive the benefit of his expertise
at some time in their career, albeit in small doses.

Unfortunately, this system did not operate as effectively
as it might have done for about a year from the end of
May 1978 until the end of June 1979, i.e. for the
whole of the final year of the experiment, because the
Head of English became Acting Deputy Head during that
period, once again a decision made by the Headmaster and
one which reflects priorities.

The decision to make class teachers totally responsible
for the teaching of English, based on the assumption that
all teachers should be competent teachers of English (as
one teacher said, 'I think all teachers are expected to
teach English'), was particularly unfortunate for the Book
Flood cohort of children in the outer city experimental
school, because none of the teachers responsible for
teaching English at 11+ or 12+ was a specialist either by
training or experience: they were specialists in Geography,
French and Music at 12+, when in-depth case studies of
teachers were conducted. The children were well aware of
their teachers' lack of knowledge and expertise, which was
reflected in the small amount of time devoted to reading
and book promotion.

One child, during a case study, stated quite categorically, and unprompted, that, while the class teachers at
10+ and the Head of English were able to recommend books
to them, it was his opinion that the class teachers at 11+
and 12+ knew very little about children's books. All the
case study children in this school told me that there was
far less time available for reading in school at 12+
than there had been at 10+. Time was devoted to the
reading of a class reader chosen for the year group by the
Head of English, to creative writing, grammatical work
and comprehension, leaving little time for book choice,
silent reading and discussion of books. Without time for
silent reading in school, many of these children would
never read, either because they did not want to read at
home, or, very often, because the conditions in their
homes were not conducive to settling down comfortably and
reading for any length of time. The children regretted
the lack of time for silent reading from a book of their
choice at the upper end of the school, and did not feel
that the class reader was any substitute:

'...when you read in the class you have got people
who aren't very good readers and they stop and they
sort of put commas in the wrong places, and full
stops, and you've just got to work it all out, and it
takes your mind off it as well'.

One of the teachers in this school, to whom I am particularly
indebted for his honesty, studied French at university;
he followed this with a Dip. Ed. course, in which a
small amount of English was included. He had hoped to
teach French, offering Maths as a subsidiary subject; he

had not reckoned with the common assumption that all
teachers are automatically teachers of English. So, when
as a class teacher of 12 year olds he was required to teach
English, he felt uncomfortable in the rôle. He believed
that his pupils were fully aware of his lack of interest
in children's literature, which lack of interest he recognised
as a disadvantage, as he was unable to recommend books
to the children; nor was he able to make an informed
contribution to any discussion about books, which a group
of avid readers who happened to be in his class particularly
looked forward to.

In the inner city experimental school, on the other
hand, although English was taught by class teachers at 9+
and 10+, the subject was taught by 'specialist' teachers
in the upper half of the school, when the English teaching was shared between the Head of English and another
teacher who has considerable knowledge of children's
literature and long experience of teaching English. Equally
importantly, the Head of English in this school was quite
clearly part of a strong team, consisting of people who
valued not only the skill of fluent reading, but also the
cultivation of a reading habit. The Headmaster had strong,
positive views about reading and the teaching of English,
views which were reflected in the allocation of staff to
English teaching, including the choice of remedial
teachers. During the final year of the experiment, when I
spent a great deal of time in each of the four schools,
it became apparent that the staff of the inner city experimental school were enthusiastic and knowledgeable about
children's literature, and indeed about literature generally, which must surely reflect to some extent the Headmaster's choice of staff.

The Head of English, as well as being a specialist by
training, was well-informed in the areas of children's
literature, reading and language development. The other
12+ teacher of English had taught in the school for
almost 30 years and was able to discuss a wide variety of
children's authors from first hand knowledge, for she
regularly read them to herself, to the pupils, and to
her young relatives. She was greatly excited about the
arrival of the Book Flood books, as were most of the
teachers in that school; for instance, the specialist
staff such as cookery, woodwork, art, etc. all wanted
their share of the 'flood', and the woodwork department
built sloping shelves to house them. This teacher also
had considerable skill in book promotion. For example,

instead of always reading an entire book to a class, she would often '...read a little to everyone and say, "There it is on the shelf!" or "It is one of a series."' Both she and the Head of English spent time talking to the children about the books they had read. This teacher's attitude, which was positive, and her enthusiasm, are best expressed by her own account of her expectations as a result of the availability of the extra books:

'The fact that there is a selection of books wider than our own school library, obviously means that they will be able to find more to read. I think a lot of the children who are fairly interested but who don't have a lot of encouragement at home, would not join a public library, if it was not at the end of their street. To go out of their way to the library is something they would probably not do, *so I suppose we should expect an improvement* - they'll read more, they'll begin to read more fluently, and, as they have exhausted what is first of all suitable for them, they'll begin to search through the shelves and begin to be a little more selective.'

So, in addition to the influx of books, the children in this school had the benefit of teachers who were knowledge-able about reading and about the content of the books, who were skilled in presentation and promotion, and who had positive expectations. They continued to set aside time for all aspects of reading until the children left the middle school; they read aloud to the children, listened sometimes to the children reading, the children were required to read parts of class readers to themselves, and they were given time for silent reading of a book of their own choice, so that the 'flood' continued to be used throughout the school. Silent reading from a book chosen, within certain limits, by the child is so important for many reasons, yet so few teachers feel that time devoted to this activity is time well-used. They need to be knowledgeable and experienced not to feel that they are being lazy if they let their pupils 'just sit and read'.

Also, many children do not enjoy a class reader; that is not to suggest that they will not get something out of it, especially if the teacher knows his books and his class well enough to choose sagaciously; indeed, this is one of the most effective ways of introducing books which pupils will enjoy but which are too difficult for them to read alone. However, they are more likely to accept it if they are also given the opportunity to read something of their own choice. It might be salutory to note some of the case study children's remarks at this point:

> 'I don't like reading a book with the teacher because they explain nearly every word and you lose track of the story.'

> 'If we read the book with the teacher she explains things to you so you forget what she's read. I think you read more with your own reading book, *because you can follow it and imagine deep inside you the characters; also when you are reading a book by yourself you can imagine a person there which is you.*'

> 'I don't really like reading a book with the whole class and the teacher because I sometimes don't like the book we're reading. I like it when we read our own books in the library because you like the book you're reading.'

> 'I like a lesson where we all read our own reading books. I don't like reading with the class taking it in turns to read because some of them are slow readers. I like reading by myself, but sometimes I like it when the teacher reads to us.'

Very few children rated the class reader very highly. Perhaps its use should be limited, and greater use made of the short story, and readings of extracts and beginnings of books, which are subsequently made available to the children, possibly in batches of half a dozen. Then, when 99% of the children were obviously enjoying the beginning of a rather difficult book being read to them by the teacher, they might well request its continuation, in which case the activity would take on the tone more of a treat than a chore, especially if the teacher read well, and avoided using the occasion to hear children read aloud or test their comprehension, any fruitful exposition being saved until the end of a chapter.

Of course, as long as some teacher training courses for those who intend to teach English have the kind of literature element described by one teacher as 'a potted 'A' level course', there is little hope of us turning out

the specialists in children's literature, in addition to
the more usual reading and language development, who are
so badly needed in our schools. The Head of English in the
outer city experimental school, who specialised in English
at college, described his college course as an extension
of the 'A' level syllabus, with no mention of children's
literature. Similarly, the teacher with responsibility
for the school library in the outer city control school
described his subsidiary English course as an advanced 'A'
level course, only applicable to sixth form teaching, yet
intended for teachers at all levels, including prospective
primary school teachers; at no time had anyone spoken
to them about children's literature. Although this does
not apply to all training courses, it is very unfortunate
that it should apply to as many as it does. It means that
having an English 'specialist' on the teaching staff of
a school is not necessarily an indication that she will
have any literature expertise below 'O' level.

TIMETABLING

    When timetabling English lessons with reading in mind,
it is important firstly to ensure that enough time is
allocated overall, so that staff do not feel that they are
hurtling through a syllabus of some kind, either to meet
the requirements of the secondary or upper school to which
the children will go next, or to get the children through
'O' level or 16+, and therefore feel guilty if they allocate
time to silent reading (although this is less likely
to happen if they believe that silent reading improves
reading skills). During the experiment the Headmaster of
the inner city control school, who firmly believed in
specialist teaching at 11+ and 12+, increased the number
of English lessons (average) per class from 4½ to 7, plus
one library lesson. With 7 lessons a week teachers can
have no excuse for not devoting at least a single lesson,
and preferably a double, to book choice and silent reading
 - preferably a double because this allows a full half
hour for concentrated reading with no interruptions, time
at the beginning of the lesson for changing books, filling
in record forms and generally settling down; and time at
the end for children to talk to the teacher and the rest
of the class about a particular book, or, as the children
become more sophisticated, for class discussion.

With too few English lessons, teachers are often tempted to relegate reading time to the end of lessons when children have completed whatever piece of work has been set, a safe way of ensuring that the high achievers, who probably read at home anyway, having the conditions and encouragement, will be the only ones to read in school also. These are some of the comments made by the children:

'We can choose books on a Friday after spellings...'

'...you can read it in school after spellings and when you have finished your work. (We get)...about ten minutes.'

'...we only have about five minutes after lessons and then we don't have another until two days.'

And that was in a school where only the most reliable, i.e. those from backgrounds where there were likely to be books anyway, were allowed to take books home.

Precisely when in the week you decide to have your silent reading lesson will vary according to the group personality of each class; I sometimes asked them which time they would like for reading, as they have an overall view of their own timetable and its effects on their collective mood which I could not possibly have. It is a mistake to slot in single English lessons at the end of timetabling leaving no space for doubles, or too many on the same day, or always placing them after swimming or games.

ROOM ALLOCATION

Room allocation is also far more important to the successful teaching of English than is commonly accepted. To quote the Bullock Report:

'one of the side-effects of the notion that "every teacher is a teacher of English" has been its extension to "my room is suitable for English"'.

Ideally, in the primary or first school and first two years of the middle school, children will be taught for the most part in their class bases, where there should be a book corner with adequate shelving, display units, and, if possible, a rug and a couple of easy chairs or

sag bags, so that children can comfortably read a few pages
of one or two books, before finally making a choice. In
the secondary school, or upper half of the middle school
and upper school, ideally English will be taught by trained
teachers in subject bases, where there will be an adequate
supply of books, both fiction and non-fiction at the
appropriate level or levels for the pupils who use the
base, or bases, if two or three specialist teachers are
involved. There will probably be a need to separate out in
some way the easier books and the most difficult, and,
within that categorisation, to arrange the fiction according
to author and the non-fiction according to topic.
Display will be of great importance; I myself try to present displays which integrate fact and fiction, to change
the displays regularly, so that they do not become part
of the wall-paper, and to actively involve children in
display, by inviting them to select a topic and arrange
books, by pinning up a wall chart where they can record
the books which they have most enjoyed, and surrounding
the chart with voluntary book reviews. Again, ideally
the bases will have a corner where pupils can choose books
in peace; for some reason we accept this up to the age of
about ten years, and in the adult public library, but
feel that it is somehow too frivolous and unworkmanlike
for the secondary school pupil.

Book posters around the walls add to the atmosphere of
the English base. Of course, display is more likely to be
successful if there are display units available. In the
Book Flood the swivel stands which are found in many book-
shops were found to be effective. In the inner city
experimental school display was facilitated by the use of
sloping shelves around the walls, made by the woodwork
department soon after the beginning of the experiment,
financed partly by the school and partly with money
provided by the Advisory Service.

A fairly typical problem arose in the inner city control
school, where there simply were not enough classrooms to
go round. One teacher was, therefore, always peripatetic
within his own school. In the middle year of the experiment
that teacher was the Head of English. In the final year
he was given a base; a room at one side of a hut, the
other room on the other side of the 'foyer' being
occupied by the remedial teacher, in an attempt to
establish some sort of 'suite'. The foyer is an extremely
grand name for a rather small, smelly entrance (with

lavatories behind it), housing a meagre stock of paper-
backs. Since it was almost always draughty as well as
smelly it hardly provided an atmosphere conducive to
browsing. Nevertheless, with scant resources, this school
managed to do a great deal to encourage reading, because
of the expertise and enthusiasm of the teachers involved,
and the positive attitude of the Headmaster, who was always ready to learn from experience and made several
important changes in the organisation of English in the
school, during and immediately after the experiment.

SCHOOL AND CLASSROOM LIBRARIES

The organisation of school and class libraries is
obviously of vital importance if reading is to become an
integral part of school life rather than something which
only goes on in certain classrooms, and only in English
lessons. There should be class libraries in tutor rooms
for short bursts of reading during tutor group periods
for older children who do not stay in a class base,
libraries in class bases for the younger children, and in
subject rooms for the older children. This means that, if
a room doubles as a tutor room and, for example, a cookery
room, there will be a collection in that room of general
fiction books, and a separate collection of books on
cookery, diet, food through the centuries, shopping and
the consumer, eating habits in different countries, etc.

This situation did, in fact, pertain in the inner city
experimental school, partly because of the additional
books made available by the Book Flood, and partly
because of the attitude of the Headmaster and his staff. I
shall deal with the attitude of the Head in greater detail
in a later section, and his attitude to school and class
libraries in particular at this point. He had, at one
stage in his own career, been responsible for a school
library. He believed that books should be borrowed and
taken home, should be found everywhere in school and
perceived as friends, and that both teachers and pupils
should devote time in the classroom to sitting and reading. Therefore, inevitably, he firmly advocated the use
of both school and class libraries. At the time of middle
school re-organization he was anxious to spend the £1000
allocated to middle schools of secondary origin entirely
on books. He moved the location of the school library
from the far corner of the assembly/gym/dining-hall to an

attractive room, which was specially refurbished, at a
central point in the school. And, most importantly, he gave
responsibility for the school library to an enthusiastic,
energetic and knowledgeable young man, who had an unusual
degree of rapport with the pupils. He also ensured that
the school library was not used for lessons other than
actual library lessons.

There was no clear-cut distinction between school and
class libraries in the inner city experimental school.
Stock was flexible; borrowing was encouraged from any
area using a uniform card index system, the emphasis
being on book use rather than book storage.

In the outer city experimental school there had been no
class libraries prior to the experiment, as the Head
believed in concentrating book resources in a centralised
stock. Whilst such a centralised stock is essential to a
school, it should be combined with books in the classroom
if time and resources are to be used efficiently. If a
child can only change a book once a week in a formal
situation in the school library less reading will be
done; also, we should bear in mind that many children
find the visit to the school library rather a daunting
experience, and, in any case, they will find it less
daunting if they become familiar with borrowing in the
more homely situation of the classroom library. Having
become acquainted with an author, and the skills involved
in book choice in the classroom, children will often go
on from there to seek out a favourite author in the school
library with increased confidence. Here are some of the
children's comments:

> '...And in the third year I didn't bother with the class
> library so much because I found a whole selection of
> Alfred Hitchcock in the school library which I
> enjoyed very much.'

> '...when you come down to the (school) library every
> week, you've got one book, and when you've got them
> in the class you can get them whenever you want, not
> just when you are told to go down to the library.'

One girl described reading during registration and not
hearing her name called, and others told me how they
made a habit of reading their class library book whenever they finished a piece of work. And, of course, this
is a wonderful practice provided it is *in addition* to a

silent reading lesson for everyone, including those who
never finish a piece of work early.

The school librarians in both the control schools were
very competent people, but were somewhat disheartened by
the lack of resources, and, in the case of the inner city
control school, by the lack of space, which often necessita-
ted the use of the school library as a classroom. The two
outer city schools were also, I believe, handicapped by
the fact that the school libraries were of the open plan
variety, and thus open to all the noise and distraction of
preparation for school dinners, choir practice, P.E., etc.
The libraries were very attractively laid out but neither
quiet nor peaceful.

THE ROLE OF THE HEAD TEACHER

Of course, when we are considering the distribution of
capitation allowance it is important to put any current
spending in the historical context for each school, i.e.
what is spent this year must be judged in the context of
what was spent last year, the year before and often before
that also. However, having said that, it is still possible,
with care, to arrive at a fairly realistic picture of the
way in which money is apportioned, and that will depend
to quite a large extent upon the head-teacher's priorities.
A case in point, already discussed, was the decision
by the Head of the inner city experimental school to
spend the whole of the £1000 allocated to him as a result
of re-organisation on books for the school library. If a
Head accepts the very significant effect which improved
standards of reading can have, not only on English achievement levels, but on the level of literacy in the school
generally, then he will not view money spent on school
and class library books as money spent for the benefit of
one department only, but as money very well spent for the
good of the entire school, provided, of course, that the
teaching staff have the encouragement, enthusiasm and
expertise to use the books to advantage, and, indeed, to
choose books sagaciously so that money is not wasted.

In all fairness, I must say that all four Heads in the
study valued reading very highly indeed; had they not done
so they would hardly have committed themselves and their
staff to a three year involvement in a piece of research
which was likely to cause considerable inconvenience and

additional work. Also, I believe, any one of them would be
prepared to do all in their power to improve facilities
with regard to reading once they were full convinced of
the efficacy of a particular method. Indeed, as already
mentioned, some such changes were made during the course
of the experiment, and it is perfectly possible that others
have been made since. I am describing the situation as I
left it at the end of July, 1979.

Although all four Heads were convinced of the importance
of developing *reading skills*, they were not all equally
convinced of the importance of children developing a
reading habit and enjoying regular reading as a hobby. For
instance, the Head at the outer city experimental school
more than once expressed the view that he saw no great
advantage in children taking up reading as a hobby. He
was certainly concerned that children should leave the
school with the ability to read with understanding, so
that they might cope with the demands of the upper school
and of the 'world outside' after school, and went to great
pains to try to ensure that this did happen; yet he saw
little connection between this aim and the encouragement
of enjoyment in reading, or of allocating teachers with
expertise and enthusiasm to those lessons which involved
reading at the upper end of the school. He also revealed
the familiar suspicion that the 'avid' reader might be
the less active, less 'sporty' type of child, who perhaps might be missing out on other aspects of life. In
fact, the case studies revealed this to be quite untrue;
in this experiment, as in the large scale American survey
reported in *Reading in America 1978*, it emerged that the
avid reader tended to be very active in all sorts of
ways, cramming a great deal of planned activity, including
television viewing, into the day; whereas the infrequent
reader tended to do very little else and was often a
rather aimless person, (of course, Whitehead et al.
(1977) and Margaret Clark (1976) reported similar findings on the high activity level of readers).

I think it is fair to say that the other three Heads
were aware of the intrinsic value and pleasure of reading
in a very personal way, but that the two Heads of the
inner city schools were more inclined to allow that knowledge to influence their choice and deployment of staff,
and not only their acquisition of books. The Head of the
inner city experimental school displayed this attitude
from the outset of the experiment, and the Head of the

matched control school increasingly so as the experiment
progressed. It was as though the experiment served both
to focus his ideas and to give him the confidence to
implement them in school. This was manifested in the
increased number of lessons allocated to English, the
provision of an English base, and the determination to
provide a better one, and, above all, in his growing determination that no one other than the well informed and
enthusiastic should be involved in the teaching of
English. He told me that, when he became headmaster, he
had set out deliberately to change the attitude of his
staff to the teaching of English, and that this was one
reason why he had offered to involve the school in the
Book Flood. He believed that some teachers regarded
English as a '...convenient lesson to fill in the timetable', so he aimed to concentrate the teaching of English
with a small number of 'specialists' at the upper end of
the school, or, at the lower end, committed junior-trained
teachers. He emphasised and frequently reiterated the
fact that he is totally committed to the idea of one or
more English specialists in the school, and stated that
he would appoint another specialist when the present Head
of English leaves, or retires. At the end of the experiment he was also using a part-time teacher on his staff,
who is an English graduate and has been a journalist, in
addition to the Head of English. He stated quite categorically
that the Book Flood had caused him to look more closely
at reading in school, and this despite the fact that his
school was a control school, and as such did not receive
any material benefit until September 1979.

Thus, this Head had in common with the Head of the matched
experimental school the determination to ensure that
English and reading/children's literature were taught by
those with the appropriate skills and the necessary
enthusiasm. What he did not share was the latter's initial
conviction that he could carry the rest of his staff along
with him until external support was forthcoming, and he
did not share the vast numbers of books. These inevitably
boosted the morale of teachers who were already committed
to the aim of inculcating a reader habit in their pupils,
and no doubt even half the quantity will have had a marked
effect in the control school. He also had fewer and older
classrooms - accommodation and resources are important,
not only in the very obvious practical ways, but also
because they boost the morale of staff and pupils, especially
those pupils in predominantly working-class, inner city

areas such as the area where both of these inner city schools
were situated. They particularly need the benefit of a large
number and wide variety of attractive books in school and
class libraries and in a school bookshop, as well as attractive, comfortable and peaceful surroundings in which to
choose those books. Unless we are prepared to commit large
sums of money to the provision of those resources and
facilities there is little point in talking about equality
of opportunity and compensatory education.

THE CHILD's POINT OF VIEW

   The pupils themselves were fully aware of the value of
reading both as a means to an end, and as a way of escaping
into new worlds, or experiencing hypothetical situations.
They were also fully aware that a number of their teachers
did not value reading as much as they did themselves, as
well as of the ignorance of some teachers as far as children's literature was concerned. For instance, one 12-year-
old boy, who was the subject of a case study, wrote:

   'We do not get anywhere near enough time for reading in
   school. The teachers, some of them, take it for
   granted that you are a good reader, just because you
   are old and in the top class. When they find out
   your're not as good as you should be you get into
   trouble, which is wrong. I was lucky because I was
   taught by my mother to read... These library lessons
   should be in the timetable. It is a very important
   thing is reading. Reading on the whole is very educational and enjoyable if you are confident enough.'

And, of course, confidence depends on skill, which depends
on the continued teaching of reading skills at secondary
school level. In conversation, another case study boy made
the following statement:

   'Most schools put reading (after the tots have learned
   to) way down the list of priorities. When we are 5 our
   teachers parade archaic *Janet and John* books in front
   of us. One of the most boring things is being told to
   sit down by a teacher and read a book that doesn't
   interest you at all.'

This 12-year-old was an avid reader, as was the other child quoted, yet both were able to sympathise with the less fluent or enthusiastic.

The children were able to volunteer information about which teachers were conversant with the books in school and thus able to recommend them and discuss them in an informed way. One child, for example, said:

> 'One was a sports teacher, one was a Maths teacher and Mr.------ used to be a sort of Music teacher. He knew about the violin and that, but he didn't tell us about books.'

This was a reference to the teachers of English in a particular year. They were also highly critical when they did not have time allocated to silent reading in school, probably particularly because many of them had little opportunity or encouragement for reading at home; and they were unanimous in their appreciation of books around them in the classroom, especially if they had chance to choose and read them. They were also appreciative if the books were carefully arranged and well displayed, if the teacher was able to introduce new authors to them, and, preferably, if the selection available was changed fairly regularly. This is relatively easy if there is mobility and flexibility of stock between all the classrooms for a certain age group.

All in all, one cannot help feeling that the pupils themselves had the right ideas about the advantages of fluent reading and the cultivation of a reading habit, as well as about the ways in which school organisation can create the right environment and provide the right sort of help.

Unless resources, physical conditions, practical encouragement from the Head, and teacher expertise and enthusiasm coincide as they did in the inner city experimental school, then all but those who were encouraged by their parents in the early years will find that the development of higher level reading skills and the establishment of a permanent reading habit are left very much to chance.

50

BIBLIOGRAPHY

1. INGHAM, J. *Books and reading development: the Bradford Book Flood Experiment.* London: Heinemann Educational Books 1981.

2. BULLOCK, A. (Chairman). *A language for life: Report of the Committee of Enquiry.* London: H.M.S.O., 1975.

3. CLARK, M.M. *Young fluent readers.* London: Heinemann Educational Books, 1976.

4. INGHAM, J. Recording children's responses to books in the Bradford Book Flood Experiment. In: BRAY, G. and PUGH, A.K. *The reading connection.* London: Ward Lock, 1981.

5. READING IN AMERICA 1978. Washington: Library of Congress, 1979.

6. WHITEHEAD, F. et al. *Children and their books.* (Schools Council Research Studies). London: Macmillan Education, 1977.

APPENDIX 1: The 'Ingham-Clift' Reading Record Form
What I Think About My Book

Your Name .... *Your Class* ....
Title of Book ....
Author ....
Date you began this book ....

ANSWER THE FIRST TWO QUESTIONS WHEN YOU CHOOSE A BOOK TO READ

(1)   Where did you get this book from? Tick one box below.

The public library .... ☐ 1
The school library .... ☐ 2
The books in the class .... ☐ 3
It belongs to me .... ☐ 4
It belongs to a brother or sister .... ☐ 5
I borrowed it from a friend .... ☐ 6

(2) Why did you choose this book?

ANSWER THE REST OF THE QUESTIONS WHEN YOU HAVE FINISHED WITH YOUR BOOK

Date you finished with this book ....

(3) Did you take this book home to read .... *Yes/No*

(4) *How much of the book did you read? Tick one box which applies to you.*

I read all of it	1
I read over half of it	2
I read less than half of it	3
I read a few pages	4

(5) *What did you think of this book? Tick one box which applies to you.*

It was one of the best books I have ever read	1
I liked it very much	2
I quite liked it	3
I did not like it much	4
I did not like it at all	5

(6) *How difficult was it to read? Tick one box which applies to you.*

Very difficult	1
Quite difficult	2
Not difficult but not easy	3
Easy	4
Very easy	5

(7) *Did you talk to anyone about this book? If you did, put a tick against the people you talked to.*

Your class teacher	1
Another teacher in school.............	2
Your friends	3
Your parents	4
Your brothers and sisters	5
I did not talk to anyone about it	6

(8) Have you told your friends that this is a
good book? ....   Yes/No

(9) Would you like to read another book by
the same author? ....   Yes/No/
                                                    Don't Know

(10) If there is anything else you would like
to say about your book, write it here.

LIBRARY SERVICES TO ETHNIC MINORITY CHILDREN

Linda Hopkins
Assistant County Librarian, Education and Youth,
Nottinghamshire County Library

Most of today's papers are concerned with specific
pieces of research, but our brief this morning is rather
different in approach. In looking at public library services
to ethnic minority children, firstly we want to bear in
mind that children's services must have regard to children as part of their families and as part of their communities, and secondly that there has been very little specific
research into public library services to ethnic minority
children.

We want, therefore, to make a rapid survey of some of
the research on public library services to ethnic minorities
(although there is not very much of it) to pin-point
some of the problem areas, particularly in relation to
children's services, and then to look at some practical
examples of library work with ethnic minority children
in one authority - *not* to hold up this authority as a
shining light, but to examine the sorts of activities
which libraries might undertake, and whether in fact they
are providing for a real need or whether they are based on
accurate or false assumptions of need.

In looking at the research then, there was a very early
article by Clare Lambert in the Journal of Librarianship in
1969, *Library provision for Indian & Pakistani communities
in Britain* (1). This was followed in 1972 by two papers to
the Library Advisory Council by Frank Sissons and Maurice
Line on library provision for immigrants (2). In the same
year, two M.A. theses were presented at the University of
Sheffield, *Library provision for Pakistani immigrants in
Sheffield: the children* and a second thesis on *the adults* (3).

A thesis was also presented by Edgar at the University of
Strathclyde on *Library services and Asian immigrants in
Britain* (4). In 1975 *Library services to the disadvantaged*
(5) was published by Bingley, which included the chapter on
'Library Services to Indian & Pakistani Immigrants in
Great Britain' by Croker. There was little else published
on this subject until 1978, when the Library Association
published *Public library service for ethnic minorities
in Great Britain* (6). This publication attempted to assess
the overall picture of what was happening around the country,
by surveying the backgrounds of minorities (i.e. Poles,
West Indians, Indians, Pakistanis and Bangladeshis,
African Asians, Chinese, Cypriots and Southern Europeans)
and by providing a statistical analysis of public library
services to six London Boroughs. This analysis includes
an outline of children's services as described by the
children's librarians, and a chapter on the local schools
and their particular attitudes to ethnic minority children,
with the language and literature issues which they raised.

This publication immediately highlights a number of
the problem areas. Firstly, that of definitions and termi-
nology. You will have noticed the gradual change from the
use of 'immigrants' when referring to Asian communities
to 'ethnic minorities'. This change reflects partly a
change of attitude as the term 'immigrants' has taken on
rather a derogatory tone and a negative image, and partly
an increase in awareness that many black and brown people
are born in the U.K. In 1982 therefore, comparatively very
few of the children of ethnic minority origin are actually
immigrants. This problem of definition, however, remains
for the researcher, in that many of the official surveys
and census returns use variable definitions (e.g. of New
Commonwealth and Old Commonwealth immigrants). A detailed
analysis of the statistical sources can be found in
Chapter 3 of Clough & Quarmby's study (6).

The second area of difficulty is the lack of accurate
and up-to-date statistics. The most recent figures in the
Clough and Quarmby book are based on the 1971 census, and
these are obviously considerably out of date. Communities,
particularly ethnic minority communities, have changed
radically since 1971.

Thirdly, there is a continuing debate, particularly in
Education, as to whether certain statistics relating to
ethnic minorities should be kept at all, because of possible
mis-interpretation and mis-use. Consequently, in 1973, the
Secretary of State for Education ceased the collection of
certain statistics in relation to ethnic minority pupils
in schools, and for children's services this will of course
create gaps in our knowledge of the existing situation.

The most recently collected statistics relating to
public library services for ethnic minorities were collected
by Madeleine Cooke for her B.N.B. Research Fund project
in 1979. Her survey *Public library provision for ethnic
minorities in the U.K.* (7) suggested that much library
provision is often based on an inadequate knowledge of
minority communities: their size, nature and needs. It also
high-lighted the tendency for provision to be made only in
areas with a high proportion of minority communities, that
is, largely in inner city areas. Yet, it is estimated that
only one quarter of ethnic minorities live in districts
where they form more than 20% of the total population (8).
Who is providing for the other 75%, one wonders? A second
major tendency highlighted by this survey was the increased
use of special grants under Urban Aid, Inner City Programme
or Section 11 of the Local Government Act 1966, to assist
with services for ethnic minorities. In particular, quite
a number of authorities have used such grants for the
appointment of specialist Ethnic Services Librarians.

The latest survey to take a look at the national picture
is a report by Pat Coleman, commissioned by the British
Library Research & Development Department, on *The public
library and the disadvantaged* (9). The report includes a
lengthy section on Services for Ethnic Minorities, as well
as sections on services to Adult Literacy, the Elderly and
Young People. Consequently, the report envisages ethnic
minority services as an intrinsic part of the general
pattern of library services, and the report is highly critical
of the existing state of services throughout the country.
The controversy which has surrounded this particular report
- the British Library's refusal to publish, and criticism
of what was referred to as its lack of objectivity -
reflects the differences in attitudes and approach still
current in this field.

At this point I want to 'lay my cards on the table' and
enlarge on what I see, both from the published reports and
from my own experience, as some of the issues that we still
have to come to terms with as a profession. One major factor
emerges: we do not know, and in some cases we do not wish
to know, our communities. We must however recognise the need
for greater involvement in our communities and the need to
make an informed and accurate assessment of community needs
for library services, instead of working on a series of
assumptions. One method of achieving this might be to use
the local community to do some of the research. For example,
the Asian Community Action Group last year published a
short report on *Library Services and the Asian community (10)*
presented to a working party run by library services in Lambeth.

With particular regard to children's services, attempts
to discover the needs of communities may bring us face to
face with another set of issues:

(a) Members of the communities will have different
     views on their children's needs. Some will be
     anxious for their children to become proficient
     in English as quickly as possible. For the schools,
     this may mean a programme of English as a Second
     Language teaching: for libraries, it may result in
     requests for 'Grammar' books, which in our view
     may run counter to current educational practice.

(b) Are we to be influenced by our local education
     authority policy in any case? Our local LEA may
     take the view that the use of mother-tongue will
     impede children's development in English, whereas
     recent research suggests that, on the contrary,
     mother-tongue maintenance assists children's grasp
     of linguistic structures in both languages, and
     also assists development of basic concepts for the
     young child who has not yet sufficient English to
     develop these in English. Is there nevertheless a
     demand from parents and children for mother-tongue
     books, even though the Education Department locally
     does not make any provision?

(c) What of the still current attitude in some quarters
     that black and brown children are just children
     and do not have special needs - the 'I don't notice
     their colour' syndrome; Eric Clough and Jackie
     Quarmby quote evidence of this in their book and

it is certainly an attitude that I have come across
in my own work. Further to this, although the
Commission for Racial Equality report *Between two
cultures* (11) recognised that generally most young
people of ethnic minority origin do wish to pre-
serve something of their own culture, some teachers
and librarians nevertheless still express the view
that black children do not want 'black literature'
because they want to be like all other children.
We must recognise, however, that a range of attitudes and influences (for example, the lack of
status accorded to a black child's culture in
school) are at work here, and that such a view
held by some people does not exonerate us from
providing a multi-cultural library service.

(d) Often when there is a discussion of special needs,
it is only in terms of Asian children, whilst
children of Caribbean origin are not considered.
Again, there is a fair amount of research now
published on the issue of the language spoken by
West Indian children in Britain and on their
educational needs.

These then, are a few of the issues we must approach
in any formulation of services to ethnic minority children.
If we can arrive at a more accurate assessment of needs we
must then be willing to respond to those needs by a commitment to provide adequate library services in terms of stock,
staffing and activities.

Is our commitment adequate? Are we providing a stock
balance which reflects the whole community? Generally I
feel that we are *not*, and this view is supported by Pat
Coleman's report - and indeed by a recent issue of the
Library Association Record, which carries the report of
disruption to a Hackney Borough Council meeting by a
group called 'The Hackney Ethnic Minority Library Con-
sultative Committee'. This Committee wished to complain
that the authority spends only 1% of its bookfund on
reading material related to ethnic minorities although they
constitute 35% of the Borough's population.

With regard to staffing, how many of our staff have a
knowledge of ethnic minority backgrounds, or indeed, how
many, if any, of our staff, belong to the ethnic minorities?

Has our authority made an appointment of an Ethnic Services Librarian and if so, do we support that Librarian, or are all other staff allowed to assume that ethnic services are provided by the 'Ethnic' Librarian and therefore that no-one else need be concerned?

I am convinced that we must ensure that services to ethnic minorities are an integral and integrated part of the whole library service, and that if we have one, the Ethnic Services Librarian should co-ordinate, initiate and promote services but that *all* staff should be involved in providing those services to the whole community.

To return to the research then, what are the current needs? Primarily, we must research the backgrounds and needs of our own minority communities. Secondly, there is very little research at present on the library needs of ethnic minority children specifically, and thirdly, we need to look further at the needs of the West Indian population in Great Britain, including the children of Caribbean origin.

To finish on a less pessimistic note, one welcome recent development has been the production, and in some cases publication, of specific local pieces of research for one or two of the schools of librarianship, notably that of the Polytechnic of London. Pirkko Elliott is here today to introduce her own report on library needs of children attending self-help mother-tongue schools in London (12), and the Polytechnic of North London has published another interesting piece of work by Jaswinder Gundara on the information needs of Indian women (13). More locally, for me, Tina Clements produced a dissertation at Loughborough University on library services to the West Indian communities, with particular reference to Nottinghamshire, Leicestershire and Derbyshire (14). The PNL School of Librarianship series of Information Sheets on library services to the Chinese and the Boat-People (15) have also proved very useful. One of the extra values, of the student research particularly, is the greater awareness that it suggests, and indeed promotes, amongst trainee and newly qualified librarians within this area of library service.

Following this paper, library services to ethnic minority children provided in the Inner Ring Zone of Birmingham were described with the aid of slides by Maggie Norwood, Children's Librarian, Birmingham Metropolitan District.

REFERENCES

1. LAMBERT, Claire. Library provision for Indian and
   Pakistani communities in Britain. *Journal of
   Librarianship,* 1(1), January 1969.

2. SISSONS, Frank. *Library books for immigrants: a paper
   submitted to the Library Advisory Council, April 1972.*
   LINE, Maurice B. *Library provision for immigrants: a
   paper for the Library Advisory Council.* Appendix A,
   LCE (72) 34, 1972.

3. CLOW, D. *Library privision for Pakistani immigrants in
   Sheffield: the children.* M.A. Thesis, University of
   Sheffield, 1972.
   DUDLEY, M.P. *Library provision for Pakistani immigrants
   in Sheffield: the adults.* M.A. Thesis, University of
   Sheffield, 1972.

4. EDGAR, J.R. *A study of public libraries and Asian
   immigrants in Britain.* M.A. Thesis, University of
   Strathclyde, 1972.

5. MARTIN, William J. *Library services to the disadvantaged.*
   London: Bingley, 1975.

6. CLOUGH, Eric *and* QUARMBY, Jackie. *Public library service
   for ethnic minorities in Great Britain.* London:
   Library Association, 1978.

7. COOKE, Madeleine. *Public library provision for ethnic
   minorities in the U.K.: the report of an investigation
   carried out on behalf of the B.N.B. Research Fund between
   January–May 1979.* Leicestershire Libraries, 1979.

8. HERBERT, D.T. *and* SMITH, D.M. *eds. Social problems and
   the city: geographical perspectives.* London: Oxford
   University Press, 1979.

9. COLEMAN, Patricia M. *The public library and the disadvantaged.* London: Association of Assistant Librarians, 1981.

10. *Library services and the Asian community: a report to
    the Working Party on library services in Lambeth.*
    Asian Community Action Group, (15 Bedford Road, London
    SW4) August 1980.

11. ANWAS, Mohammed. *Between two cultures; study in the relationships between generations in the Asian community in Britain*. London: Commission for Racial Equality, 1978.

12. ELLIOTT, P. *Library needs of children attending self-help mother-tongue schools in London*. London: School of Librarianship, Polytechnic of North London, 1981 (Research Report No.6).

13. GUNDARA, Jaswinder. *Indian women - information needs*. Occasional Publication no.2, School of Librarianship, Polytechnic of North London. London: Polytechnic of North London, 1981.

14. CLEMENTS, Christine. *The West Indian community in Britain and the relevance of the library service to their needs; with particular reference being made to the East Midlands*. Dissertation, Dept. of Library and Information Studies, University of Loughborough.

15. *Library needs of the Chinese in London*. Information Sheets 1-18. School of Librarianship, Polytechnic of North London. March 1980.

LIBRARY NEEDS OF CHILDREN ATTENDING MOTHER-TONGUE SCHOOLS

Pirkko Elliott

Research Assistant,
School of Librarianship,
Polytechnic of North London

Research into the library needs of children attending self-help mother-tongue schools in London has been undertaken by the Polytechnic of North London as part of a research programme into library needs of minority ethnic groups. Other projects in this programme have been a general study of library services to ethnic minorities (1), and specific studies of Cypriots (2), Armenians (3), supplementary education schemes (to be published as an appendix to the report of the project described here), and the library needs of Chinese in London (5). This last project, which is financed by the British Library, will come to an end at the beginning of 1982, and the results will be published soon after.

Several research methods were employed in the project on mother-tongue schools (4). Two of these were taped interviews in English, and mother-tongue interviews that were not taped; other methods used will be mentioned here, with some of the results and conclusions. By mother-tongue school is meant a voluntary organized class or classes in which children of ethnic minority origin are learning their mother tongue or acquiring literacy in their mother tongue.

Ten mother-tongue schools in four London boroughs were visited, covering Bengali, Chinese, Greek, Gujerati, Italian, Polish, Punjabi, Spanish, Turkish, and Urdu. Whenever possible ten children between the ages of seven and sixteen were interviewed in each school. The interviewing of children had not been used before to find out about children's library use and needs in this country, although it had been used to interview children in general in social work studies.

Interviewing children and taping these interviews worked well; children were not inhibited by the machinery nor were they too worried about the confidentiality of the interviews (each child was of course assured that the tapes would be listened to by myself only, and after transcribing they would be wiped clean). The major advantages of this method are that taping gives the freedom to digress, and that the interviewing process is more natural than if the interviewer takes notes or writes down answers. In any case this would have been impossible during most of the interviews because of the speed with which the children were speaking.

The piloted interview sheet had 34 questions, and each interview lasted about ten minutes. All of these children, regardless of age, were asked the same questions. Among the questions asked were those concerning reading in English, in mother tongue, speaking in mother tongue, story telling by parents or other relatives in English and in mother tongue, library use, reading preferences by type of material, and O-level aspirations.

In order to deal with the possibility that children might become over-enthusiastic and exaggerate, a number of checks were built in; specific titles of books that had been read by the children were asked for, and also a short summary of the books that they had read.

The second type of interviews were those conducted in mother-tongues. These were carried out in ten languages: Arabic, Bengali, Finnish, Greek, Gujerati, Japanese, Latvian, Norwegian, Tamil, and Turkish. Ten children in each of these ten languages were interviewed. On the whole the children in the sample, that is children from ethnic minorities between the ages of seven and sixteen who attended mother-tongue classes, spoke English more fluently than their mother-tongue. The questionnaire used for these interviews was shorter than the one for the taped interviews. All the mother-tongue interviewers were given the same set of instructions; they encountered hardly any problems despite the fact that there was not much time available to train them. Any interviewers employed, however, should be given a thorough briefing.

THE MAIN RESULTS

In all 200 children were interviewed, of whom 189 said that they could read English. Of the 189 pupils 172 had actually read a book in English in the previous few months. 124 out of the 200 said that they could read in their mother tongue. 121 of these pupils had read a book in their mother tongue in the same period.

NUMBER OF BOOKS READ BY THE PUPILS IN THE MOTHER-TONGUE SCHOOLS IN THE GIVEN PERIOD

	Mother-tongue	English
Arabic (10)	5	4
Bengali (20)	11	15
Chinese (10)	8	8
Finnish (10)	7	10
Greek (20)	12	18
Gujerati (20)	5	17
Italian (10)	6	10
Japanese (10)	5	6
Latvian (10)	9	10
Norwegian (10)	7	9
Polish (10)	10	9
Punjabi (10)	8	10
Spanish (10)	8	10
Tamil (10)	1	9
Turkish (20)	14	17
Urdu (10)	5	10
TOTAL	121	172

This shows a considerable variation in the numbers of mother-tongue books read by the children of different language groups.

The most popular sources for English books were school or class libraries, (just over one-third), whilst for mother-tongue books it was the mother-tongue school or the linked community library (about one-half). A more detailed break-down follows:

SOURCES FOR BOOKS READ IN ENGLISH AND MOTHER TONGUE

	E	%	MT	%
Public library	40	23.3	2	1.7
School/class library	59	34.3	–	–
Shop	41	23.8	15	12.4
Gift	22	12.8	9	7.4
Loan from friend	7	4.0	2	1.7
M-t or community libr.	1	0.6	61	50.4
Abroad	–	–	12	9.9
No source given	2	1.2	20	16.5
TOTAL	172		121	

From these results it seems that public libraries represent an underdeveloped resource. I shall return to this point.

Other elements of this research were the drawing up of as complete a list as possible of mother-tongue classes in London, in order to try to establish their range and nature. I also aimed to find out how many of the schools had mother-tongue collections, and whether there was any co-operation or contact with public libraries. To this end a short questionnaire was sent to 210 mother-tongue schools. Detailed information was received from over 130 of these schools. Over half had mother-tongue collections, some schools had librarians looking after their collections, and only a handful had direct contact with public libraries. Teachers in mother-tongue schools were interviewed, and public libraries of the four boroughs in the investigation were visited in order to discuss their policies for mother-tongue provision.

In all, 330 schools covering 33 languages were located, with over 40,000 children attending. Most of the children used libraries of some kind; public, school/class, or community/mother-tongue school library. It seems that the number of children attending mother-tongue schools is at present on an upward trend, and there must be an even larger potential audience for mother-tongue provision among the children who do not yet attend mother-tongue classes.

Over half of the children interviewed were literate in their mother tongue, but it is a remarkable fact that only two mother tongue books read by the children in the sample came from a public library. Many of the children interviewed, however, visited public libraries fairly frequently for English language books.

Some of the implications of this research are: first, more books in mother tongues with an appropriate background and setting need to be published urgently. Primarily this is a problem for publishers, but librarians could nonetheless influence the speed and the type of publication that is needed. These new books and existing published materials need to be acquired by school and public libraries. Second, librarians should reconsider their whole policy concerning the location of their mother-tongue collections and the issuing of mother-tongue materials. At long last it seems that mother-tongue teaching within school curricula is catching on. This is an additional reason for more published books. Third, this particular research project will we hope make librarians more aware of the potential numbers of readers with a mother-tongue other than English. Fourth, in the process of this research I found a considerable amount of co-operation between different types of institutions which deal with the area of mother-tongue provision, such as the Linguistic Minorities Project, the NCMTT, the ILEA, and many minority ethnic groups themselves. Consequently, researchers and practitioners in the area were more aware of other research and work going on in the field of mother-tongue provision than is perhaps customary in research in general.

REFERENCES

1. CLOUGH, E. *and* QUARMBY, J. *A public library service for ethnic minorities in Great Britain*. London: Library Association, 1978.

2. LEEUWENBURG, J. *The Cypriots in Haringey*. London: Polytechnic of North London School of Librarianship, 1979.

3. SABBAGH, R. *Armenians in London*. London: Polytechnic of North London, School of Librarianship, 1980.

4. ELLIOTT, P. *Library needs of children attending self-help mother-tongue schools in London*. London: Polytechnic of North London, School of Librarianship, 1981 (Research Report No.6).

To be published:

5. WEY TSE CHIN, *Library needs of Chinese in London*. London: Polytechnic of North London, School of Librarianship.

6. WELLUM, J. *Afro-Caribbean supplementary education schemes in London*. London: Polytechnic of North London, School of Librarianship.

THE ROLE OF THE NATIONAL BOOK LEAGUE
IN RESEARCH INTO CHILDREN'S LITERATURE
AND ACTIVITIES CONCERNED WITH
CHILDREN'S BOOKS

Beverley Mathias
Children's Book Officer,
National Book League

The National Book League is an organisation concerned
with the promotion of reading and the use of books for pleasure.
As such it is the only book organisation not concerned
with the interests of a specific trade or professional group,
or with commercial gain. This aspect of the National Book
League is known to most people in any way connected with the
book world. It is the other aspect of the National Book
League, the effect the organisation has as a catalyst and
a research organisation, that needs to be mentioned specifically today.

Many of you will be aware of the best seller lists,
the booklists, exhibitions, displays, speeches, book awards,
etc. which are connected in some way with the National Book
League, but how many know that the same organisation was and
is also involved in the Bedford Square Book Bang, the Bradford Book Flood, the National Book Committee, LIBTRAD, IBBY,
the School Bookshop Association, the report on school book
spending, Children's Book Week, and other actions designed
to help capture and interest hitherto uninvolved people who
just might become readers if approached in the right way.
This is the catalyst action of the National Book League.

To help in the promotion of books is important, to
interest children in reading is vital, to stimulate and
encourage those who work with children and adults in the book
world is necessary to the survival of the industries and
professions connected with the printed word. Even with all
of this emphasis on doing things, on being involved, on
encouraging others to be involved, there is yet another
field that needs to be explored and assisted in whatever
ways are possible, and that is the field of research. So

what can the National Book League do to help?

Today we are concerned predominantly with children's books and the literature with which children become familiar. To do that we need to be concerned with those who work with children, who teach them to decode the printed symbols, who encourage them to read for pleasure, who introduce them to books, who read to them, tell them stories, in fact every person who has anything to do with putting a book and a child together in any way at all. If this is going to be done to the best advantage there are certain things which must be known. We need to find out what children read, where they obtain it, how they find out, who shows them, why they read, who produces the material and why, if it is 'good' or 'bad', if it is readily available, what other people say about children's books, the alternative methods of teaching reading, the ways of introducing books to children, the ways of running libraries, the cunning methods employed to help children to see that books are fun and not something to be feared. To sum up - to raise the awareness of children's books as a necessary part of every child's life.

This is where the Centre for Children's Books at the National Book League comes in. Since 1966 there has been a reference library of children's books at the National Book League, there have been a number of people involved in the library, and each person has contributed a great deal to the development, publicity and use of the services offered. Now we are able to offer a little more through the generosity of the Arts Council and the continued support of children's book publishers, plus other individuals and organisations which finance the National Book League.

All services to and for children are now grouped under the umbrella title Centre for Children's Books, and it is this expansion and extension of services that I would like to detail. I would like to show some ways in which these services can be used to expand your knowledge of children's books and the children's book world, how the services can act as a stimulant to research, and an encouragement to those who feel that children's books are a necessary and integral part of every child's growing process.

The Children's Reference Library I have already mentioned briefly. It holds one copy of every children's book published in this country, for a period of 24 months. Each

publisher sends a copy prior to, or at, publication date.
These are then catalogued and shelved for a 24 month period.
The result of this is that at any one time there are some
7,500 books on the shelves. At the end of that period they
and the relevant catalogue cards are removed. The cataloguing
is quite detailed. The library needs to give more than just
author/title information if it is to offer more than the
average public library. So every illustrator is listed,
including the jacket illustrator, and in addition, for mov-
able and pop-up books, the paper engineer is given. If you
were to enquire for *Robot* we could find it in the catalogue
via the title, the author/illustrator (Jan Pienkowski), or
the two paper engineers who executed the mechanics (James
Roger Diaz and Tor Lokvig). At the moment there is no
subject index, but as the Dewey system is used that does
not present too many problems. The shelf arrangement is
much the same as you would expect to find in any children's
library. The fiction is shelved by author, the non-fiction
by Dewey decimal numbers, using the revised Dewey for
British schools. We do pull out the story collections and
shelve them separately, since we find that many teachers
want to look at them as a group and it is much easier to
separate at the point of cataloguing. The picture books
present problems, as they do in any library. We have face-
out display shelving, the remainder are shelved spine out
in pigeon-holed shelving which helps to keep them tidy.
Because we need to be able to find any book as soon as possible the picture books do need to be kept in order. At the
moment we are experimenting with an arrangement by title
plus special sections of moveables, board books, paper-
backs, early readers, and very small books. If this arrangement proves to be unsatisfactory we shall try again.

The shelving in the library is interesting - Terrapin
Reska standard shelving, but in bright yellow. It is
deliberately in the lower price range available, and is 4'8½"
high - an international standard for children. This means
that we can not only shelve the books more successfully,
but we can also show one of the ranges of commercial
shelving available for children's libraries. We do receive
quite a few enquiries about the shelving. The picture book
shelving is adapted from periodical shelving and works well.
The same type of shelving is used for the periodicals, but
with the flat shelves moved as close as possible to each
other so that we can store two years of periodicals in
sight. The periodical collection is reasonably comprehensive;

we subscribe to or receive gratis over forty periodicals,
journals and papers connected with children's literature.
They range right through the spectrum from productions
on roneo sheets to professional journals. All are extremely
valuable. Amongst the publications received are *Top of the
News* (ALA), *Orana* (Australia), *Horn Book* (USA), *Material
Matters* (Herts), and *Books for Keeps* (SBA). All periodicals
received are held for two years, some are then cut for
articles before being discarded, others are kept indefinitely.
We hold complete files of *Signal, Growing Point, Children's Literature in Education* and *Books for Your Children;*
and extensive files of *Horn Book* (from 1954) and *Junior
Bookshelf* (from 1946). Some of the post-war developments
in British children's books could be traced through the
lead articles in *Junior Bookshelf*. One of the earlier issues
has a marvellous article about a new illustrator, Harold
Jones, who is currently having a retrospective exhibition
of his work. Through *Horn Book* you can read acceptance
speeches for the Newbery and Caldecott medals, the various
May Hill Arbuthnot lectures and many other interesting and
important articles. Nancy Chambers has now collected many
of the best articles in *Signal* into one book, but by looking
through the back issues you can find what people thought
about a book or an author at the time when both were perhaps controversial or new. With the Arts Council grant we
have been able to employ a person part-time to index all
journals not indexed annually, and to abstract articles of
interest from newspapers and some unlikely sources. In this
way we have been able to pick up a very interesting interview given in New York by Maurice Sendak on the subject of
his new picture book *Outside over there,* and to find other
small mentions of children's books and surveys which might
otherwise have gone unnoticed.

There is a small but comprehensive selection of materials
about children's books - criticism, history, bibliographies,
biographies, promotion of books, storytelling, use of books,
and other topics of interest to those who are involved in
the field of children's literature. Again, although the 400
volumes shelved in the library are current material, there
are around 300 volumes which are kept in the archives.
These are of immense value to anyone researching children's
literature and wanting contemporary material and opinion.
Some of these titles go back to the 1930's. The collection
in the Children's Reference Library should be used as an
adjunct and a complement to the Mark Longman Library at the
National Book League, which is a specialist library about

books. It is the Mark Longman Library which holds all books
concerned with the history of illustration and the history
of children's literature. A short bibliography of some of
the books added to the two libraries in the past year is
included below. Some are well known, others may be less
familiar; all are available for use. Also at the National
Book League, but part of the Mark Longman Library, are three
collections of illustrations; the Leslie Linder Collection
of Beatrix Potter originals, the Arnrid Johnstone Collection
(she drew some of the very first Puffins), and the Diana
Stanley Collection. This last holds all of the Worzel
Gummidge drawings, the illustrations and some of the jackets
for The Borrowers series, and also the manuscript for one
of the Borrowers stories.

Grace Hogarth has given Eleanor Farjeon's own collection
of the famous *St Nicholas Magazine* to the National Book
League. These can be seen in the Children's Reference
Library. They cover the period 1883 to 1900. If you have
not had the opportunity of seeing these they are well worth
a look. Some of the illustrations have been handcoloured
by Eleanor Farjeon.

A new collection is the Signal Poetry Collection. Through
the generosity and work of Nancy and Aidan Chambers we have
a growing collection of in-print poetry for children, along
with a small collection of works on the use of poetry. The
stock numbers some 600 volumes at present. This is catalogued
by author/selector and by title. All poetry withdrawn from
the current library collection will be added to the Signal
collection. We hope that this will encourage and stimulate
the use of poetry in schools and libraries and will also
draw attention to the vast range of poetry available for
children.

The British Section of the International Board on Books
for Young People has given a collection of British published
works of Hans Christian Andersen. This is not complete but
is intended to be a representative collection only. Earlier
this year a publisher generously gave a magnificent Danish
Album of Hans Christian Andersen which contains beautiful
colour plates of letters, documents, stories, photographs
and drawings.

We are slowly building a collection of reference books
for children. At the moment this includes a few sets of

encyclopaedias (amongst them a new Junior Britannica), some dictionaries and an atlas. Books suitable for inclusion will be added as they are withdrawn from the current shelves. This, we hope, will be particularly useful to teachers trying to build a reference collection on a small budget. Most bibliographies of current materials are held in the Book Information Service, but the Centre does hold a guide to British secondary schools, press guides, and the *Subject guide to children's books in print*.

There is a small but growing collection of award-winning children's books. These are limited to British awards, but hopefully the collection will continue to grow and prove to be useful. We feel it is necessary to have this sort of special collection so that all awards can be seen alongside each other. Current award winners are always displayed in the library. Each year we prepare a list of award winners, listing the major ones and giving the year of inauguration.

The Centre for Children's Books receives many foreign visitors, and one of the pleasing results of these visits is the contact with other countries and the small parcel of books which often arrives a few weeks after the visit. For a while nothing was done about these, but they are now shelved by language in the library. Many are translations of British books, some are books which we know by translation, and it is interesting to see the differences in production and the ways in which the same story can be told. The collection now includes books from Japan, India, Germany, Australia (in 5 languages for multi-racial communities), Holland, France, and soon the Republic of China. Again it is important for these to be available for people to see, particularly those involved in multi-ethnic community work.

One of the most important developments in the field of children's books at the National Book League has been the development of information files. These are still in their infancy but are already proving to be a valuable aid in answering enquiries and giving information about books, authors and other aspects of children's literature. There is a slowly growing file of biographical information on authors and illustrators, including some photographs. The general information files include all sorts of information that might one day prove useful; there are lists of films available for hire, audio visual catalogues, foreign language catalogues, information about local and overseas organisations concerned with books, promotion material from libraries and schools, special lists prepared by libraries and other organisations such as the National Children's Bureau, and notes of special collections.

What of the future? In addition to continuing all that has been started, and improving on all services as time and finances allow, it is intended that there should also be a small amount of publishing. The National Book League is already well known for its book lists and exhibitions. The Centre for Children's Books at the National Book League has produced *The Authors and Illustrators List* – over 200 authors, illustrators and poets who will attend book events, together with information on the booking of speakers, running events, where to go for finance, and what fees one can expect to pay. The Centre also produces a periodical list annually, giving subscription details and a brief resume of content for each periodical, journal or paper received in the Children's Reference Library. The next publication we hope will be a guide to the children's book world. The exact content and style are still under discussion. A further venture is the attempt to build up an information file on all the special collections of children's books held throughout the British Isles; not only early children's books, such as the Wandsworth Collection, but poetry, twentieth century fiction, and other collections.

The work of the Centre is not all concerned with the production of files, neat shelving of books and comprehensive cataloguing. It also offers help and assistance in a variety of ways. Many enquiries come through the mail and by telephone. These are dealt with promptly. Some enquiries may necessitate a visit to a school, library or other organisation; others may need to be encouraged to visit Book House and use the Centre themselves once they have been told of the help available there. The promotion of books and the encouragement of children to use books for pleasure is always of paramount importance. Everything that is done is to this end. Some of the pleasures gained from this promotion work are the delight of children and teachers when they first have a book event at school, the teacher who goes away from the library with a list of books to buy for the school, the student who after working every week on her thesis came back to say thank you and to tell us she had passed and had a job, the parents and the children who wander in to look, read, and share the enjoyment of a book. All of this is what we are working for. The facilities are there, some still developing, but they are a waste of valuable time if they are not used. This is what the National Book League is doing to help in the work of promoting, using and researching children's literature.

BIBLIOGRAPHY

1. KOCH, Kenneth. *Rose, where did you get that red? teaching great poetry to children*. New York: Random House, 1974.

2. KOCH, Kenneth, et al. *Wishes, lies, and dreams: teaching children to write poetry*. New York: Random House, 1980.

3. WILLIAMS, Miller *and* CIARDI, John. *How does a poem mean?* New York: Houghton Mifflin, 1975.

4. DUKE, Judith S. *Children's books and magazines: market study*. New York: Knowledge Industry Publications, 1979.

5. LOWE, Susan. *The original artwork and manuscripts of Dromkeen*. Melbourne: Melbourne State College.

6. BAUER, Caroline Feller. *Handbook for storytellers*. Chicago: American Library Association, 1977.

7. MARSHALL, Margaret. *Libraries and the handicapped child*. London: Andre Deutsch, 1981.

8. HEARNE, Betsy *and* KAYE, Marilyn. *Celebrating children's books*. New York: Lothrop.

9. CHAMBERS, Nancy. *The Signal approach to children's books*. London: Kestrel, 1980.

10. TUCKER, Nicholas. *The child and the book*. Cambridge: Cambridge University Press, 1981.

11. ARMOUR, Jenny. *Take off...* London: Library Association, 1980.

12. BUTLER, Dorothy. *Babies need books*. London: Bodley Head, 1980.

13. HEEKS, Peggy. *Choosing and using books in the first school*. London: Macmillan.

14. HEARNE, Betsy. *Choosing books for children*. New York: Delacorte, 1980.

15. CHILDREN'S BOOK COUNCIL. *Children's books: awards and prizes*. New York: Children's Book Council.

16. CROUCH, Marcus. *Chosen for children (1977)*. London: Library Association, 1977.

17. KIRKPATRICK, D.L. *Twentieth century children's writers*. New York: Macmillan, 1977.

18. SUBJECT GUIDE TO BOOKS IN PRINT: New York: Bowker, 1948.

LIST OF PARTICIPANTS

Jan ADAMS	London Borough of Southwark
Marie ADAMS	South Eastern Education and Library Board, N. Ireland
Brian ALDERSON	School of Librarianship, Polytechnic of North London
Jillian ALLEN	Central Library Resources Service, I.L.E.A.
Helen ARMSTRONG	Royal Borough of Kensington and Chelsea
Beryl ARNOLD	London Borough of Hounslow
Keith BARKER	Westhill College, Birmingham
Ann BARLOW	Goldsmiths College, University of London
Miriam BENNETT	London Borough of Ealing
Moyra BENNETT	Central Library Resources Service, I.L.E.A.
Virginia BERKELEY	Bedfordshire County Library
J.A. BOOTH	London Borough of Hammersmith and Fulham
Margaret BRIGHT	London Borough of Havering
Winifred BRISCOE	London Borough of Enfield
Marian BURFORD	London Borough of Waltham Forest
Veronica DORSET	North Westminster Community School, I.L.E.A.
Pirkko ELLIOTT	School of Librarianship, Polytechnic of North London
Jean FARLEY	London Borough of Southwark
Helen FARRAR	Central Library Resources Service, I.L.E.A.
Margaret FEARN	Dept. of Library and Information Studies, University of Loughborough
Angela FLETCHER	London Borough of Richmond upon Thames

Ruth GARDNER	American Community Schools Limited
Sally GIBBS	School of Librarianship, Leeds Polytechnic
Lesley GILDER	Centre for Library and Information Management, University of Loughborough
Morag GOLDFINCH	London Borough of Newham
Dierdre GREENWOOD	St. Pauls' Girls School
Myra GRIMES	Institute of Education, University of London
Elizabeth HARRISON	Suffolk County Libraries
Christine HEADLONG	Oxfordshire County Libraries
Pauline HEATHER	Centre for Research on User Studies, University of Sheffield
Jennifer HIBBERD	Cambridgeshire Libraries
Veronica HOLLIDAY	Hampshire County Library
Linda HOPKINS	Nottinghamshire County Library
Kay HOPWOOD	Hertfordshire Library Service
Ferelith HORDEN	London Borough of Wandsworth
Jennie INGHAM	Middlesex Polytechnic
Joan JEFFERY	London Borough of Islington
Barbara JONES	Knowsley Metropolitan Borough, Lancs
Mary JONES	London Borough of Camden
Anne JUDSON	London Borough of Southwark
Frank KEYSE	College of Librarianship Wales
Laura KING	Central Library Resources Service, I.L.E.A.
Gillian KIRBY	London Borough of Wandsworth
Derek LOMAS	Department of Library and Information Studies, Manchester Polytechnic
Patricia LUMB	London Borough of Redbridge

Pamela MANLEY	National Youth Bureau
Philip MARSHALL	Nottinghamshire County Libraries
Beverley MATHIAS	National Book League
Joyce MEARS	London Borough of Ealing
Nick MOORE	British Library Research and Development Department
Lesley MORELAND	Toy Libraries Association
Margaret MORTIMER	Edinburgh City Libraries
Irene MUIR	British Library Research and Development Department
Frances NEWTON	Surrey County Library
Maggie NORWOOD	Birminghamshire Metropolitan District
Keith OSBORNE	Nottinghamshire County Library
Margaret PARKER	Cambridgeshire Libraries
Ted PERCY	Buckinghamshire County Library
Stephanie POTTER	North Westminster School, I.L.E.A.
Sheila Ray	Department of Librarianship, Birmingham Polytechnic
Susan REEDER	Croydon Public Libraries
Anne REILLY	Glasgow District Libraries
Linda REYNOLDS	Nottinghamshire County Libraries
Lorna ROBERTS	Westminster Public Libraries
Harry ROBERTSON	Essex County Libraries
Jan ROOTS	London Borough of Bexley
Paula ROULINSON	Cambridgeshire Libraries
Kathleen RYAN	Bolton Metropolitan Authority
Michael RYAN	Buckinghamshire County Library
Eleanor von SCHWEINITZ	School of Librarianship, Polytechnic of North London
Grace SHAW	Bolton Metropolitan Authority
Paula SIMPKIN	London Borough of Camden

Liane SOUTHCOMBE	London Borough of Camden
Tom TARRY	Lancashire Library
Viv WARREN	East Sussex County Library
Jean WATTS	The Sheppey School, Sheerness
P. WHITEHEAD	London Borough of Hammersmith and Fulham
Bob WILKES	Metropolitan Bradford Libraries
Tony WINSLADE	Derbyshire County Library
Glenys WILLARS	Leicestershire Libraries and Information Service